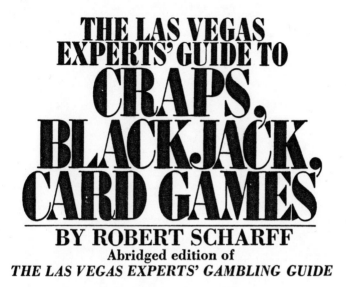

THE LAS VEGAS EXPERTS' GUIDE TO CRAPS, BLACKJACK, CARD GAMES

BY ROBERT SCHARFF

Abridged edition of
THE LAS VEGAS EXPERTS' GAMBLING GUIDE

GROSSET & DUNLAP
A NATIONAL GENERAL COMPANY
Publishers · New York

A Castle Books, Inc. Edition
Distributed To The Trade
By Book Sales, Inc.

(Abridged edition of *THE LAS VEGAS EXPERTS' GAMBLING GUIDE*)

Grosset & Dunlap Special Edition 1970

Published simultaneously in Canada

Printed in the United States of America

Contents

THE LAS VEGAS EXPERTS' GUIDE TO CRAPS, BLACKJACK, CARD GAMES

1

♠

How to Survive
(and Perhaps Prosper)
in Las Vegas

Just after Desert Inn opened in 1950, a sailor (his name is still unknown) at a craps table made twenty-seven passes in a row, which means that he won twenty-seven times in a row. The sailor, a timid man, walked off winning $750. If he had left his original bet on the table, instead of pulling money out after each win, he would have won, if he had been fantastically lucky enough to quit at precisely the twenty-seventh pass, $268,435,456. As it was, this freakish achievement (the odds on twenty-seven passes in a row are 12,467,890 to 1) nonetheless cost the Desert Inn $150,000 from the side bets that were made by bettors at the table. Zeppo Marx, of the original Marx Brothers, won $30,000, and one patron who could not get near enough to the table to make a bet, offered $500 for a grandstand position. Nobody took him up. The sailor disappeared into the desert, but the dice he used repose to this day on a velvet pillow in a showcase in the Desert Inn's lobby, a kind of Las Vegas Crown Jewel.

This incident does not prove very much perhaps, but it does prove that despite the alarming stories in your Sunday newspapers, often written by people who have never thrown a pair of dice in their lives, you *can* win at Craps or at Roulette or at Blackjack or even at the slot machines. Organized gambling is based upon strict mathematical probabilities. The house does not always win—witness the case of the sailor—but in the long run it wins inexorably. The house is *reasonably* secure behind its odds. In the long haul,

7

they know that they are going to end up with a fair percentage of the money that crosses the table. They would just as soon you did not risk a pile on those long odds, because they have a nasty habit of paying off every now and then.

Everybody who gambles wants to win. According to Sam Landy, Las Vegas' famed Professor of Chance, 95 per cent of those who try it at the "Entertainment Capital of the World" would be ecstatic if they could make enough to pick up the tab for their meals, food and drinks, and maybe have a couple of silver dollars jingling in their pockets on the way home. After all, they had a ball, and it did not cost a nickel. They are the ones who play it cautious. They are thinking of the bills, and when the risk gets too great, they draw down. It is better to be safe than sorry.

What about the other 5 per cent? They are the ones, Sam says, who come to Las Vegas to win "important money." These are the characters who give the pit bosses the shivers. They know the odds, too, but they do not play with them; they bet against them. When the weak sisters are pulling their money back, these guys are pouring it on. When they win, it is damaging.

Do you have to be a millionaire to bet this way? No, says Sam. You can start with any amount: a dollar, five dollars, a hundred, or even a dime. It is a good idea to have a little bankroll to carry you over the rough spots, but with a fair amount of luck at the first, you do not need it.

There was a doctor from Des Moines who proved just that a few months back. He had been cleaned to the tune of $40 in one of the local card rooms. That was the total amount he had allocated himself for gambling, and, as it was gone, he excused himself from the table and started to leave the casino. He had exactly 25 cents left in his pockets. The doctor was running his fingers over his last quarter as he walked by the slot machines near the door, when the thought occurred to him, "If I'm going to be wiped out, I might as well do a thorough job of it."

He put the quarter in a machine, pulled the handle and watched disinterestedly as the three wheels sprang into action. Thunk . . . thunk . . . thunk . . . JACKPOT! Thirty-five dollars worth of quarters spewed down the chute. The good doctor realized he had to make a decision. He could take the $35 and leave. This would pull him all but $5 out of the hole. On the other hand . . . He had a hunch! He took his money to the roulette table and started playing, $5 at a time. When he hit, he let it ride. In a matter of minutes, he had $1,500. He moved to the craps table, where the action is faster, and started pushing the money out again. Two and one-half hours later the doctor from Des Moines left the casino. Only this time his mood was different. He had won $27,500, and he kept it!

The secret is, the doctor was willing to gamble. He could have taken his slot machine winnings and gone home only $5 light, but he took a chance and it paid off. This kind of thinking is not so preposterous as it might seem. For example, you go to the races and you bet the favorite every time for the first seven events, and every time he runs out of the money. Now comes the eighth and last race. Do you bet the favorite again, or do you put your money on the long shot? Certainly, the risk is far greater on the long shot, but if it comes in you are home free.

Now, do not construe this to mean you should always bet your cash on the long shot. Everyone has either experienced or heard of "lucky streaks" when those one-in-a-million chance numbers come up several times in succession. If you happen to be there and have your money down in the right place, you can make a fortune. But those formidable odds are against you. It might be just your luck that when you have your chips on the long shot, it will not come in at all. That might be the time when those dice, or the cards or the ball on the roulette wheel are making up for their previous "oversights," so as not to make a liar of the theory of probabilities.

Those odds that work against your having a winning streak have their effect upon the house, too. In fact, a greater effect, because you are a short-term gambler and therefore much more susceptible to "streaks," while the house, with its much greater volume of activity, feels the full weight of the law of probability. Theoretically, the house should win just as many bets as it loses, and nobody is going to invest in any kind of business on that basis, whether it be in a gambling casino, a drug store or a steel mill.

How do the gambling houses insure a return on their mountainous expenses? Not by cheating, because the risk of getting caught by Nevada's vigilant gambling control agencies and losing everything is much too great. And besides, it is highly unnecessary. How then?

Know the Odds and Probabilities

A casino makes its money because in most of its games skill cannot be of any real help to you. All the games except the card ones, are based upon chance, and regardless of what bet you may make, the casino pays off at less than true mathematical odds. You might say this is the "commission" the casino gets for running the game, taking the risk and providing all those other attractions that bring fifteen million visitors to Las Vegas each year. John Scarne, in his book, *Complete Guide to Gambling*, points out very succinctly how this operates.

Suppose, Scarne says, that you walk up to a carnival wheel with $15 in your pocket. The wheel is numbered 1 to 15, and the operator pays off winners at 10 to 1 odds. Suppose that you bet the same number every time for fifteen spins of the wheel, and the wheel hews strictly to probability and stops on that number one time out of the fifteen spins.

You have bet fifteen and won ten. The $1 you bet on the winner was returned to you, so you have a return of $11 for your $15 investment. The operator of the wheel made $4 on the transaction, which is his charge for running the game. If he had paid you at the true mathematical odds of 14 to 1, you would have broken even . . . and so would he. "This," Scarne says, "is what makes gambling operators rich and most players poor."

From this comes the amazing revelation that it is the winners who pay for the privilege of gambling, not the losers. When you lose your money at the table, it remains there and may be called upon moments later to pay off a winner. The casino actually is just a middleman for this kind of money. But when you win, the house chops off a percentage by paying you off at less than the mathematical odds. In doing so, the casino has made a profit on the transaction. This is exactly the same as "markup" in any other type of business, where a merchant buys his commodities wholesale and sells them retail. The difference in price pays all his expenses and overhead and, he hopes, gives him a reasonable profit.

This profit is known as house *percentage* or *advantage*. This percentage, or tax, is subtle, but it is always there. Let us say that you bet $1 on each toss of a coin—an even money proposition. But, instead of paying you $1 every time you win, the house pays only 99 cents, and when you lose it collects $1. That gives the house an advantage, or profit, of 1 per cent. While this seems like a minute amount, it could mean that if, at the end of a 1,000 tosses, you had won 500 and lost 500 of them, you would be out $5. It is possible, in the case of big house advantage bets, that even when a player has a lucky streak and wins, he ends up a loser. His chance to clean up has been greatly reduced because of high percentage.

The house percentages vary from game to game and bet to bet. Players who do not know what percentages they are up against do not realize that they are often paying much more for the privilege of gambling than they need to. The smart player avoids games and bets having high percentages against him. The table below indicates the range of house percentage in the more popular casino games:

Craps		0.83 to 16.7%
Blackjack or Twenty-One	(expert play)	Under 1%
	(average play)	2 to 3%
	(poor play)	6% and up
Roulette		5.27 to 7.9%
Slot Machines		10 to 50%
Keno		20% and up
Bingo		Over 20%
Money Wheel		11.1 to 25.9%
Chuck-a-Luck		7.9 to 22.2%
Baccarat		1.06 to 1.23%
Faro		1.57%

The betting limits—both minimum and maximum—vary from casino to casino and game to game. For example, in Casino Center the minimum bet at Craps is 10 cents, at others 25 cents, while at all Strip casinos the minimum is $1. The exceptions to the $1 minimum bet at Strip games are slot machine play, with 5 cent, 10 cent, 25 cent, 50 cent, and $1 machines; Roulette, which has a 25 cent bet on the numbers; and Baccarat which has a minimum of $5 to $20. The Strip hotels have a maximum of $2,000 at Baccarat, $1,000 at Craps, and $500 at Twenty-One. At Craps, the maximum flat bet is $500 when odds of $500 are taken as well. At Blackjack, the maximum bet can be made again on split hands, and another $500 can be made on a double down play. There is, however, no maximum or minimum limits on your play, except if the table is closed for any reason. Slot machine play, Craps, Blackjack and Roulette are open on a twenty-four-hour basis. You can gamble for as long as your money holds out. Also there are no limits on the amount of money you can win, except the capital available to the casino. No player has ever "broken the bank at Las Vegas." In Nevada, unlike Monte Carlo, each table does not close down if it is "broken." Here, to "break the bank," one would have to break the entire house. And the odds against that are nearly impossible.

Speaking of odds, many players, including inveterate gamblers, confuse them with "chance," thinking that they are one and the same thing. But they are not. Chance is the possibility or probability of winning a bet you make, while odds give the difference or ratio between the chances of winning and not. In other words, it is the probability of failure in a given risk compared to the probability of success. The first figure given in an odds ratio is always the one for the probability of failure. A success probability of one chance in ten is the same as odds of 9 to 1. Actually, odds are given in order to equalize a wager that would otherwise be unfair.

In stating the odds of certain games, especially Craps, you must watch for the words "to" and "for." This psychological trick of some casino managements can cost you money if you are not careful. For instance, the meaning of the odds of 15 *to* 1 is that the winning payoff is fifteen betting units plus your initial bet—a total of sixteen units. Odds of 15 *for* 1 indicates that the winning payoff is fifteen units including your initial wager. In other words, you are receiving odds of 14 *to* 1.

In most of the casino games, the player *takes* the odds. That is, in a 2 to 1 situation, for instance, he takes the two units if he wins or pays one if he loses. In other words, the majority of the time he is on the "long end" of the odds. There are a few times, in Craps, for example, when it is possible for the player to lay the odds. In this instance, he is on the "short end" of the odds, say 5 to 11, which means that if he wins he receives five units from the house or when losing, gives up eleven.

ODDS TO PERCENTAGE PROBABILITY

Odds	Percentage Probability	Odds	Percentage Probability	Odds	Percentage Probability
Shorter than 1–100	Quasi-certitude	1–2	66.667	9–2	18.182
		8–15	65.217	5–1	16.667
		4–7	63.656	11–2	15.385
		8–13	61.905	6–1	14.286
		4–6	60.000	13–2	13.333
1–100	99.010	8–11	57.895	7–1	12.500
1–50	98.039	4–5	55.556	15–2	11.765
1–33	97.059	6–5	54.545	8–1	11.111
1–25	96.154	10–11	52.381	9–1	10.000
1–20	95.238	20–21	51.220	10–1	9.091
8–100	92.593	Evens	50.000	100–9	8.257
1–10	90.909	21–20	48.780	100–8	7.407
1–9	90.000	11–10	47.619	100–7	6.542
1–8	88.889	5–6	45.455	100–6	5.660
2–15	88.236	5–4	44.444	18–1	5.263
1–7	87.500	11–8	42.105	20–1	4.762
2–13	86.667	6–4	40.000	22–1	4.348
1–6	85.714	13–8	38.095	25–1	3.846
2–11	84.615	7–4	36.364	33–1	2.941
1–5	83.333	15–8	34.783	40–1	2.439
2–9	81.818	2–1	33.333	50–1	1.961
1–4	80.000	9–4	30.769	66–1	1.493
2–7	77.778	5–2	28.571	100–1	0.990
30–100	76.923	11–4	26.667		
1–3	75.000	3–1	25.000		
4–11	73.333	100–30	23.077		
2–5	71.429	7–2	22.222	Greater than 100–1	Insignificant chances
4–9	69.231	4–1	20.000		

Almost every scientific study of gambling starts with an analysis of what occurs when a coin is spun, and we shall do the same. Unless bias is in any way present, the chance that the result will be *heads* will nearly be equal to the chance that it will be *tails*. But, every spin is independent of another, and there is no more likelihood of a *head* turning up following a *tail* than there is of another *tail*. Even if *tails* turns up twenty times in succession it will not be in the slightest astonishing for the sequence to remain unbroken with the twenty-first spin. True, many players think that a *head* is more likely to turn up than *tails* because they believe that "law of averages" states that *heads* and *tails* must eventually come up an equal number of times. Let us emphasize one very important fact: the theory of probability, or law of averages, is just a mathematical prediction of what may be expected to happen in the long run, not a law that says that certain things must inevitably happen. Thus when you toss a coin, the theory of probability says that *heads* will turn up approximately half the time in the long run. It does not say that in a very long run *heads* and *tails* must come up exactly the same number of times.

Statistical coin-spinning experiments have indicated that the difference between actual and expected results often increases over long runs. For instance, in a series of one hundred spins, the results may be forty-five or fifty-five *heads* rather than the expected fifty. If the number of tosses were increased to 10,000, the deviation between actual and expected results may have increased to fifty under or over the predicted 5,000. In the first case, the percentage of deviation was 10 per cent (5/50), while in the second, the difference percentage was only 1 per cent (50/5000). As you can see, the percentage of deviation between the actual and expected results does tend to decrease in the long run. But it is only in this sense that the results seem to "even up."

Failure to understand the theory of probability costs many players a chance to win "big" money. Let us see how this affects the casino and the individual player. Since the casino makes so many more bets than any one player in a single gambling session, the house experiences a much longer run and thus its wins and losses will usually conform rather closely to what the theory of probability says it can expect. On the other hand, the individual player, even in an extended series of gaming sessions, could be considered only a short run. His winning and losing, therefore, may vary a great deal from his long-run expectation. This is the fact that many players fail to realize. That is, when they are on a "hot," or winning, streak, they are afraid to ride with it because they believe the chances of a "cold," or losing, streak setting in are constantly increasing. Likewise, when losing steadily, they insist on continuing because they think the "law" states that the longer they lose the more certain they can be that their fortunes are bound to change. Remember that a game of chance is just that, a game of chance. If there were any sure knowledge, it would not be "chancy." As long as every roll, spin or card has many possibilities, who is to know for sure what is going to happen?

It is important, however, to keep in mind that there are definite ways to increase your chances of winning. And you *can* win at Las Vegas. But how can this be possible when:

1. *The house has a mathematical advantage on every bet you place.* This is very true because as you will see in the following chapters the house never pays off at true odds.

2. *Because of this mathematical advantage, the house stands to win from a half-cent to over 20 cents on every dollar you bet.* Again, this is a correct statement since the house's percentage is a tax taken out from the money wagered.

3. *Theoretically you lose this amount every time you place a bet.* Another statement that is true because of the house's built-in advantage. But even though you are betting constantly with the percentages against you, it is possible to beat the house during your stay in Las Vegas by judicious play, good money management, a little luck—and the theory of probability.

If you stay at the gambling table for an extended period of time, you will in all probability lose. Gambling casino operation is based, as stated previously, on the theory of probability too, and the fact that if millions of dollars of wagers are made the house will make a profit which is in direct ratio to the percentages it has in its favor. For instance, if $20,000,000 is bet over a period of a year and the overall house's percentage is 1½ per cent, the casino is *pretty certain* of netting a profit of $300,000. You note that we said pretty certain. Because nothing is mathematically improbable, a house pitted against unlimited capital over an indefinite period of time *could* run into a series of losses that would break it. Several of Las Vegas casinos have gone bankrupt.

Remembering that all things are possible, here is a supposition that is worth thinking about. If a thousand "expert" gamblers took about $25,000 and interminably made wagers against Las Vegas casinos, several of the gamblers would go broke within a few weeks. A couple would go on as long as they lived. A few would last six months or so, a few would last only a year. The majority, according to computer tests, would last for five to ten years and from time to time would be ahead of the game until that inevitable last time when the house advantage would break them. Actually, the two things that knock an expert player off eventually are the house's percentage and prolonged losing streaks. Obviously it behooves the player to select a game in which the house advantage is least against him and manage his money properly until Lady Luck comes along.

Luck and Hunches

Understanding luck is an integral part of gambling. Unfortunately, it is a very intangible thing. One modern-day dictionary defines it as "that which happens to one seemingly by chance." In an ancient Roman dictionary it might have been termed "the result of the gods." But, whatever definition you use, it plays a most important part in gambling. Actually, many of the casino games—Craps, Keno, Slot Machines, Roulette, Chuck-a-Luck, Wheel of Fortune, Baccarat, Faro—are based on just pure luck. Even Blackjack, Pan and Poker in a casino are games of luck, but since you are given some choice in your play, your skill will have an effect upon the amount that you win or lose.

Luck seems to run in cycles. There are times when nothing goes right and times when everything is favorable. Thus, many times gambling is a "matter of proper timing." It is "good luck" when you are on a winning streak; "bad luck" when experiencing a losing cycle. It is the element of the unknown—whether a cycle, good or bad, is beginning or in the process of ending—that adds extra excitement to the sport of gambling.

Human emotions such as hunches and superstitions play a major role in gambling, too. When in a game of Craps, for instance, a shooter picks up the dice, all the other players throw immediate glances in his direction, and if they like his looks, or if the shooter wears something attractive, or they like him for any one of a hundred different reasons—reasons which, in the end, prove to be just plain hunches—they will bet accordingly. You would be surprised at the reasons players give for betting certain ways.

During my many stays in Las Vegas, I have met several players who actually felt a sort of personal relationship with the dice. After a long losing streak, they would demand new cubes, complaining that the old ones had it in for them and were losing on purpose. It is very important to know that the two dice cannot *see, hear or smell*. Dice cannot remember who shot them last or what number was thrown last. Nor do they know what number will come up in the next throw, for that action is in the hands of Lady Luck. But players often imagine certain things that the dice can and will do because of certain emotions or happenings around the table. If the dice hit a player's hand, for instance, the shooter will blame him for a 7 showing up, for according to the shooter, a 7 will always come up when the dice hit a player's hand. (Well, almost always.) Or if a player is really doing well, and should his wife join him at *this moment*, he is bound to lose on the next roll, because wives have been known to be "death" to a husband.

Do not laugh at all this. You will probably pick up a superstition or two during your gambling days. *All* gamblers believe in luck despite the fact that we know that mathematics, probability and the odds are all with the house. This belief in luck and a universal wish to control it—or at least keep it—is what is at the root of most popular gambling superstitions. For instance, my wife, when she plays a slot machine, raises her left foot, because in the past she has hit several jackpots in this manner. Asinine, of course, but I do have my lucky sports jacket which I *must* wear while I gamble in Las Vegas casinos.

Does superstition have any influence on gambling? Yes and unfortunately it is usually to the depredation of the player. That is, he will often defeat himself once he gives full sway to a superstition. And once a gambler loses complete control of a situation and has allowed anything other than *good* play techniques to influence his judgment, he is bound to lose.

If your superstitions do not affect the logic of play, by all means keep them. They are a part of gambling. Sam Landy, who has an excellent collection of stories of gamblers' hunches and superstitions, tells about a woman who followed every move made by a drunk at a gaming table. Every time the inebriated one placed a bet, she would put her own right alongside. This went on for several plays, and finally a companion asked the woman: "Why do you watch that drunk and make every bet he does?"

"Because," the lady answered, "they tell me the Good Lord takes care of fools and drunks, so I'm with him!"

It might be unfair to the "science" of parapsychology to include the subjects of extra-sensory perception (ESP) and psychokinesis (PK) in the section on superstition and luck. In recent years a great deal has been written on what influence these subjects will have on the gambling industry. While believers in ESP and PK make great claims, casino owners have not yet noted any decrease in profits because of parapsychology. If you believe in ESP and PK, that is fine, but do not let it interfere with good play practices.

Every player has hunches, and so do the casino bosses. If you think that you are immune to them, then either you have an extremely analytical mind, or you have never been carried away by the super-fast action and nerve-wracking excitement of casino games. While it may be good, on rare occasions, to play your hunches, do *not* let them control your play. Gamble with a clear mind, a mind uncluttered with your emotional feeling, intuitions and superstititions. And while there is a certain amount of luck involved in all gambling, never substitute it for your knowing the game—the rules, the betting, and the percentages. You will find that you will win more often.

Good Money Management

If you expect to win *big* when Lady Luck is on your side, you must know how to manage your money correctly. "There is no question about it, proper management of your money is the most important part of gambling," according to Las Vegan Rod Morris. Rod presumably knows, since he not only is a veteran dealer himself, but an operator of the Nevada School of Dealing, which trains the employees of many of the casinos.

Before starting any gambling venture in Las Vegas, as previously stated, set an *absolute* limit that you are willing to lose. This sounds like a rather easy rule to follow, but the cashiers' windows at the casinos are usually plagued by players who wish credit beyond the limits they themselves set. Remember that this limit was established on the basis of your sound judgment under rational circumstances, and any attempt to increase this amount upon the depletion of your betting funds during the rigors of play is an emotional reaction of poor judgment. Never embarrass yourself, or the credit manager, by asking for a further extension of credit once you have reached the limit you set for your losses.

Incidentally, this limit should be an amount that you will not miss if you lose, or an amount that you would consider as spent on entertainment. That is, never bet the mortgage payment on the house or money for the baby's shoes. In order to become a "smart" player, you must have a worry-free mind. And you cannot have a clear chain of thought if you are playing with money you are afraid of losing. Therefore, be sure that you can afford your losses *before* you lose.

It is a good idea to divide your budgeted gambling capital between the various planned gaming sessions prior to your arrival in Vegas. In other words, set aside so much money for each day's gambling session rather than possibly blowing your entire limit quickly and spoiling your entire trip. Many people divide their daily sessions into four one-to-two-hour segments: morning, pre-dinner show, in between shows, and post-midnight show. This leaves the afternoon free for golf, swimming, and the many other outdoor activities available. But remember that it takes a degree of discipline to follow a predetermined limit for the entire gambling trip, for each individual day, and for each proposed gaming session. Failure to follow any part of your gaming capital plan will effectively circumvent your entire plan and can result in a frustrating time. While Las Vegas is the fun capital of the world, it can be a most exasperating place without gambling stakes.

All casino games except slot machines and Baccarat use chips rather than cash. Your money can be changed into chips directly at the playing table, but there is no provision for any change in cash and you will receive chips for the entire amount. Personal checks and travelers checks, on approval of the credit manager, will be cashed by the casino cashier in either cash or chips, or any desired combination. For all chip denominations of $5 or more, the chips are legal tender in Las Vegas. They will be accepted without question at any other casino, store, or even as a contribution at the church of your faith. The metal tokens, however, are limited in use to the issuing casino. All chips and tokens can be cashed in at the casino cashier's cage. The exception to this is the colored chips used at the Roulette layouts which are handled exclusively at the table where they are issued.

At the start of any gaming session, keep your bets small until you test your luck. If that nebulous female we call "Lady Luck" is on your side, increase your bets accordingly. On the other hand, if you lose six or eight bets in a row, stop for a couple of rounds, change tables, or go for a walk. Always press your luck when winning; never when you are losing.

Failure to follow this simple rule is why the casinos can afford such lavish furnishings and offer such fabulous entertainment. Most visitors to Las Vegas follow this rule in reverse. The average tourist generally has a fixed gaming trip and session limit in mind and does keep his first few bets small. But, after losing three or four bets in a row, he begins to have an uneasy feeling. After all, he plans to spend a week in Las Vegas and must start winning some big money soon. So he gets an inspirational hot flash and doubles his bet because the "law of averages" says that he is certain to win. The result of the next round is the same—he loses. Thus, he triples his bets in order to recoup all his losses with a win. After a few bets like this his gaming session limits are reached. He does not, however, stop; he continues to increase bets until all his Las Vegas trip capital is gone. Thus, in possibly less than an hour's time, he has ruined his planned week's stay in Las Vegas. This is a true story; it happens hundreds of times a day. Do not let it happen to you.

It is wise at the beginning to keep your single bets from 3 to 5 per cent of your total gaming session capital until you start winning and are playing with house money. By betting this percentage of your capital until you begin to win, you will not be wiped out before you have had a run for your money, and it is large enough so that you have an opportunity to win big. In other words, this arrangement provides you the opportunity to weather unfavorable runs of reasonable length, while still providing sufficient money to capitalize on a favorable streak should one occur.

Your dilemma is, of course, that no one can predict when a good run will begin; and, once a good streak has begun, it is impossible to say when it will end. But, as soon as you go ahead of the house, begin to increase the size of your bets. Thus, your object is always to get to the position where you are able to make big sum bets. To make such bets with your own money could be disastrous. But when using house money it is a different thing, so bet big.

Sam Landy tells a story that is most apropos: "Several years ago, a friend of mine went to the crap table and started with $500. In a few minutes, he was down to $40, and although he was a wealthy man, he was disturbed. The dice came around to him, and I asked to shoot the dice for him, so he gave me the 40 bucks. In those days, the house limit was $200. Well, I held the dice for one hour and five minutes. After the hand was over, I had won over $10,400 and had $2,600 on the table when I lost the hand. I won that money not because I am any *luckier* than him, but because I had the *guts, especially with someone else's dough!*"

The moral of Sam's story is simple: When playing with house money (*someone else's dough*), bet with plenty of nerve (*guts*). It is almost impossible to win "big" money if you stay at the same level bet after bet. Suppose, for example, you won ten bets in a row. Ten bets in a row at $1 each would be, at even odds, $10 winnings. But if you let the money ride until you reach the limit of the house (generally $500), you could win $1,012.

While letting the winnings ride on the table, or parlaying it, until the house's limit is reached is the quickest way to win big money, most smart players prefer the "safer" slow progression system. This is a method to get you into a progressive betting pattern during favorable runs, and allows you to bet accordingly. It is interesting to note that when big winning streaks do occur, they take place for a player over a period of time *usually* not exceeding twenty minutes. The remainder of the average gaming session normally shows a loss, or a small profit at best. The laws of probability do not call for unusual favorable runs to occur often, so be sure to capitalize on them when such situations do arise. Never walk away from a winning streak.

To see how the slow progression system operates, let us suppose you are a $2 bettor. Your original bet is $2. If you lose, continue your $2 bet. If you win a hand, bet $4. If you win again, bet $6. If you win the next bet, wager $10. If you win the $10 bet, stay at the same amount for the next. If you win again, jump your next bet to $15 and stay at this limit until you lose a bet. Then revert back to your $2 bet. Always revert to your original wager after each bet you lose. For instance, if you lose on the second bet, which was $4, return to your $2 wager on the next one.

In this manner, you become a $15 bettor when winning and a $2 bettor when losing. You are more relaxed playing this way than betting $15 when losing and $2 when winning. Most small bettors feel uncomfortable when 'making high wagers. The average $2 player is generally most happy and grateful to win a few hundred dollars now and then. This is a good take for the average Las Vegas tourist and can be done if the money is bet and managed properly. Incidentally, only about 1 per cent of the players that gamble in Las Vegas ever reach or bet the $500 limit.

The following is a table showing the progression of consecutive *winning* bets for players at various established bets:

If You Are Betting	*Slow Progression of Winning Bets*
$1	$1, $2, $3, $5, $5, $8, $10 *
$2	$2, $4, $6, $10, $10, $15 *
$5	$5, $10, $15, $25, $25, $35, $50 *
$10	$10, $20, $30, $50, $50, $75, $100 *
$25	$25, $50, $75, $125, $125, $150, $200 *
$50	$50, $100, $150, $225, $225, $300 *
$100	$100, $200, $300, $400, $400, $500

* Stay at this limit until you lose a bet. Then revert to your original bet.

By playing a slow progression, you will notice that after winning two hands in a row your profit takes care of the third bet. The next winning hands in succession are all free hands and you are not supplying the money. You will also note that the fourth and fifth bets are the same amount. This is a sort of cushion if you win both of these bets. Should you lose the next wager, you will be in a comfortable position when you start with your original bet again. Some players call this their "playing money," while others "lock-it-up." In other words, the latter players take the locked up money out of the game; not to be gambled again. Really, this money is the player's profit. It can only be considered a profit, however, when the money *leaves* Las Vegas. How many times have you heard of the big wins that are ultimately lost back to the casinos? Therefore, when you decide to lock up a portion of winnings—a smart player always does—make certain that money gets home. A check mailed there with the proceeds of your winnings removes any temptation to give it back to the casino and is a wonderful souvenir which could help bring you back to Las Vegas on your next vacation trip.

While it is a good idea to take your profit out of the game, never "drag down" as long as you are winning when employing the slow progressive system. Therefore, do not try to guess when you are going to lose. You cannot. If you start guessing, it will be your downfall. Remember that every round is a new hand. Forget the previous play—win, lose or draw. If you have made a mistake, forget about it. There is nothing you can do to rectify it now. Do not let it interfere with playing the next round or hand.

In playing a slow progression system, should your hand in Blackjack, for example, call for doubling down or splitting pairs, do not hesitate one bit regardless of what amount you are betting; you must play the hand, not the money. That is, proper play should never be affected by the size of the wager. When you have a large bet staring you in the face, just remember how you accomplished this—only one way: by playing and managing your money properly. You may lose some bets, but win others. When betting house money be brave, when betting your own be a coward. This is the key to winning important money at a casino. In other words, increase your bets during a favorable run, and avoid increasing bets during an unfavorable streak.

A smart player, as stated earlier, follows one adage religiously, and that is to make sure he is always getting the best possible odds. Select a game which offers you close to a 50 per cent chance of winning. Information on the odds and how to use them to the player's best advantage are fully discussed in the remaining chapters of this book. Be sure to follow the advice given, because good play goes hand in hand with proper money management. Also, it is easy to let the many casino distractions interfere with playing concentration, which can affect the control of your money, too.

The player who has trained to use the methods described in the following chapters *must* be able to keep his attention on the game. Casino owners will tell you, with complete candor, that their establishments are designed to inhibit your judgment and to subtly encourage an emotional approach to gambling. For many first-timers, the initial impact of the casino atmosphere is too much for them to cope with. Thus, it is most important to follow the suggestion given on page 11 to the letter. Actually, it is a good idea before beginning any gaming session to walk about the casino, observe game play, make some *mental* bet and study player reactions. But, once you are fully acclimated to the casino environment and decide to begin your gambling session, give your complete and undivided attention to your game. If you cannot do this, then do not play at that time.

During play, avoid social talk with your fellow players. Do not annoy the dealers with small talk. Most of them do an excellent job of patiently putting up with the gripes and barbs of idiots, who try to camouflage their losses and incompetence with their big mouths. If you cannot concentrate at one table because of other players' idiosyncrasies or distractions, relax a few minutes and try a new table. It is generally wise to limit your gaming session to an hour or two. Serious gambling is a tiring sport, and fatigue can cause costly errors. If you feel tired, stop play. Put your money away and come back when you feel well rested and mentally alert. Remember that action is available in Las Vegas twenty-four hours a day.

It is wise to vary your play to include more than one type of casino game. One of the reasons that Baccarat has become such a popular game is that it offers a fine break and relaxation after playing Craps and Twenty-One.

Do not drink excessively while gambling because your judgment is seriously impaired. Your senses are dulled and you are unable to calculate wisely or swiftly. Therefore, save your drinking for afterwards, either for celebrating a win or consoling a loss.

Before leaving the subject of money management, there is one more point. Do not be a "happy loser." In all Las Vegas casinos, you can find a player who spends $50 in slot machines, then suddenly hits a $10 jackpot. After a free drink on the house, he puts $10 right back into the same winning machine. As he leaves the premises, he remarks with a big smile, "Oh, well, I didn't expect to win anyway. Just came down to pass some time away, and I figured I'd spend about $50."

You would be surprised how many people make that or similar remarks, and not only around the slots, but also at the Blackjack table or the Roulette wheel or Craps table. So, to all the people who come to Las Vegas with the avowed purpose of losing $50 or $100 we will say, on behalf of the casino owners in the city, "Welcome, sucker: Come again, and come often—as often as you can." There is an old expression around the casinos that goes like this: "Show me a happy loser, and I'll show you an idiot!"

2

♠

Craps—An Ancient Game Gets a New Shake

Egyptians, Babylonians, Greeks, and Romans of antiquity all enjoyed dice games. Craps is the favorite of serious gamblers because (1) it is a fast-moving game, and (2) it gives the shooter almost even-up odds for his money (244 to 251). In addition, the craps table layouts, such as those found in the Las Vegas casinos, give the player an infinite variety of exciting side bets in addition to the basic game.

Craps, of course, is played extensively anywhere that dice can be rolled on a flat surface. True, most people begin shooting Craps at private games for coins, or maybe bills, with their fellows. But, just in case you have never played the game at all or are a beginner, we will start with the fundamentals of play.

You throw a pair of dice, two perfectly square cubes, bearing dots 1 to 6 inclusive. Should the dots total 7 or 11 on the first roll, you win your bet, and the throw is called a "natural." If the dice add to 2, 3 or 12 on the first roll, it is "craps" and you lose. You keep the dice, however, and throw again.

When you as the shooter win, it is called a "pass." When you lose, it is called a "miss." This is not always, however, determined on the first roll. Instead of a "natural"—7 or 11—or a "craps"—2, 3 or 12—a 4, 5, 6, 8, 9 or 10 may appear. Then, any such number becomes your "point" and you try to "make the point" by rolling it again before a 7 appears. Here, 7 is no longer lucky. Also, 2, 3, 11 and 12 have no meaning when you are attempting to "make the point." You keep on shooting until you "pass" by bringing up the needed point or until you "miss" by rolling a 7. If you "pass," you win, keep the dice, and start a new sequence of rolling the dice for a pass or miss.

Casino Craps

Craps as played in a Las Vegas casino is known as "Bank Craps." That is, the house banks the entire game and players cannot make side bets among themselves. The casino takes all bets and runs the game according to a definite set of house rules.

The game itself is played on a rectangular table approximately 3½ feet wide by 12 feet long, with the playing surface about 12 inches below the raised sides. The tops of the sides are grooved to make it easy for the player to store his chips. The table layout is symmetrical and provides two identical betting areas with a common center area for proposition bets.

Craps Table Layout

At first look, a craps table layout appears quite complicated. After a thorough examination, you will see that it is not so intricate as it appears because all craps table layouts in Las Vegas contain the following marked areas:

Pass Line. Any wagers placed in this area bet that the shooter is going to "pass." If the shooter makes a natural on his first roll, or throws his point before making a 7, he wins for all pass line bettors. If the shooter throws a craps (1–1 or 1–2) or "sevens out" before repeating his point, he loses for all pass line bettors. The house pays even money (1 to 1) on all winning pass line bets. By the way, the pass line is generally called the "front line" by inveterate gamblers and casino personnel.

The only time you should place a bet on the pass line is before the come-out, or first, roll for a new point. It is a mistake to make a wager on this line while the shooter is attempting to make his point since you lose the opening chance of winning on a 7 or 11. Most times, one of the dealers will inform you of your error. However, you should check whether a shooter is coming out with a new

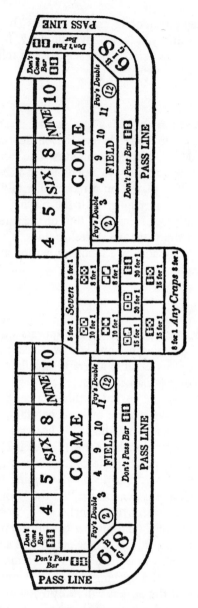

Craps table layout.

point or not by noting the marker, or puck as it is called, in front of the dealer. If the shooter is coming out, the puck will be off the layout and will have "off" written on the top of it. When the shooter is trying for his point, the puck is on the point number with the "on" end showing.

Don't Pass Line. When placing a bet in this section—often called the "back-line"—you are wagering that the shooter is going to lose. If the shooter throws a 2 or 3, or "sevens out" before repeating his point, you and back-line bettors win. If the shooter makes a natural on his first roll, or throws his point before tossing a 7, he and his back-liners lose. The house pays even money on all winning don't pass line bets.

On the don't pass section of the layout, you will note the word "bar" and two dice showing 12. This means that when betting on the back-line, should a double six come up, the bet is off; neither the house nor the players win. It is a standoff, push or tie. You may leave your bet there or remove it as you please, but there is no payoff. Don't pass wagers are made before the come-out roll.

Come. This is one of the most interesting features of Craps. Here is where you can have your own private game against the house. Let us say, for example, that when you enter the game the shooter point is 9. Before his next roll you place your bet on come. On this roll, the shooter throws out an 8. Eight then becomes *your* point. The dealer then moves your bet to 8 in the boxes above the come line. This means that you want the shooter to make an 8 before he makes a 7. If he does, you win; if he does not, you lose. When the come bet is won, it is returned to the come line and is paid off. You should be alert to remove any portion of your bet and winnings as desired before the next roll. Remember that the point for each come bet is separate from the pass line wager and is not affected by the pass line action.

Actually, you can place a bet on the come line on every roll except when a *new* shooter makes his first roll. In this case, the pass line essentially means the same as the come line. On subsequent rolls, however, you can no longer place a bet on the pass line but may make come bets. In reality, a come bet is almost the same as a pass line bet, because on the first roll for come bets as the first loss for line bets, 7 and 11 are winners, 2, 3, and 12 are losers.

Whenever your come bet points are repeated, you win. The odds (1 to 1) are the same, too.

Don't Come. The don't come area is reverse of the come section and the same rules apply as on the don't pass bets, including bar 12. As with the come bet, the first roll after you place your wager in the don't come box is your own personal game, regardless of what is happening on the rest of the table. If the dice show 2 or 3, you are a winner; if 7 or 11 come up, you are a loser; and in the case of 12, you have a standoff with the house. If a point is made, the dealer will place your bet in the back section of the box numbers, signifying that you are a back-liner. If a 7 is rolled before the point is repeated, you win; otherwise you lose. Actually both don't come and don't pass bettors are wagering that the shooter is going to lose. The house pays even odds to don't come winners. While pass and don't pass bets cannot be withdrawn after the come-out, come and don't come wagers can be removed at any time before the roll.

It is interesting to note that when a player bets along with the shooter, it is called a "right" bet. When he bets against the shooter, it is a "wrong" bet. In Craps, the terms "right" and "wrong" have nothing to do with ethics or morals, nor does it mean that a player has guessed right or wrong, so far as winning is concerned. "Right" and "wrong" apply strictly to the type of bet —with the shooter or against him.

Field. When you play the field, you bet on 2, 3, 4, 9, 10, 11 or 12 being rolled. Most casinos pay double on 2 and 12; even money on the other numbers. A few layouts substitute 5 for 4 in the field. A field wager, of course, is a one-roll bet. This means that your wager rides in the field for *only* one roll. That is, each roll is a deciding roll; you win if any of the field numbers appear, or lose if any other number shows.

Big 6 or 8. Here, you simply put your bet on one or the other. If your number (either 6 or 8) comes up before a 7, the house pays even money. Big 6 or 8 are not one-roll bets.

Any 7. When you bet in this section, you are saying that the next roll will be a 7, otherwise you lose. This is a one-roll proposition and the house pays 5 for 1 (4 to 1).

Any Craps. You are betting that 2, 3 or 12 comes up on the next roll of dice. This is also a one-roll bet and the house pays 8 for 1 (7 to 1)

Hard Ways. These are long shots, exact combinations you bet on to come up—namely 2–2, 2–1, 3–3, 4–4, 5–5, 5–6, 6–6. While this is not a one-roll bet, you win only if the numbers come up as such. You lose if the same number comes up any other way—or if 7 comes up. The odds are not uniform for all hard way proposition bets, but the payoff in *most* casinos are as follows:

Combinations	Payoff
1–1; 6–6	30 for 1 (29 to 1)
6–5; 2–1	15 for 1 (14 to 1)
3–3; 4–4	10 for 1 (9 to 1)
2–2; 5–5	8 for 1 (7 to 1)

In the preceding information on payoffs, you note that we used both the words "for" and "to." This is one of the psychological tricks of the casino management. There is a very big difference between stating odds on the basis of "for" instead of "to." The meaning of odds of 30 for 1 is that, on winning, the payoff is 30 units including your initial bet. You are thus receiving odds of 29 to 1. In a similar manner 15 for 1 is 14 to 1; 8 for 1 is 7 to 1; and 5 for 1 is 4 to 1. In practice, the original bet is left on the layout unless you request its return, and the payoff is on the "to" basis. Most craps tables in Las Vegas are marked with "for."

Casino Craps Play

On the player's side of the table you will find a casino employee known as a stickman. It is his primary job to return the dice to the shooter after each roll. He also calls out the. dice roll result and places the proposition bets. Some even act as a barker of sorts calling out the proposition bets, because these wagers have a very high house advantage and account for the major portion of the house winnings. On the opposite side of the table, in a restricted area known as the "pit," are the two dealers, one for each end of the table, and a boxman. (When play is heavy, two boxmen may be employed to speed up the game.) The dealer's prime task is to make change from cash to chips, and to collect and pay off bets on his end of the table. The other dealer provides the same function at the other half of the layout. The boxman is the final authority at the table. He carefully follows the game play, handles all called bets that are not marked on the layout, and is the arbitrator if any disputes arise.

Before the first roll of the dice by the shooter—called a *come-out roll*—bets are made by placing the wagers on layouts. As a rule, $1 is the minimum at Las Vegas Strip casinos, while downtown a minimum can be as low as 10 cents.

The stickman begins the action by offering several dice to the shooter who selects two dice. The shooter then throws the dice toward the opposite end of the table so that they bounce off the backboard, and the outcome of the roll is determined by the total of the face-up sides of the dice. The reason the stickman requests that the dice hit the backboard is so that there is no possibility that the fall of the dice can be controlled. It is extremely difficult for an expert to control the dice even if the backboard is not hit; but this caution is often made by the casino personnel because other players feel somewhat cheated if a losing roll does not follow the proper procedure. In most casinos, however, the toss is still considered legal if it does not hit the backboard.

Should the casino personnel be suspicious of a controlled roll, they might call "no dice" or "no roll," if the shooter does not hit the backboard. But only the stickman or a dealer can make the call and they do so under only very unusual situations. The term "no dice" means that there will be no decision on the roll in question. Incidentally, when one or both the dice leave the table during a roll, we have an automatic "no dice" situation. Also the dice that drop off the table are removed from the game. The reason for doing this is to minimize the possibility of introducing biased dice into the game. Of course, the casino can change the dice at any time, but seldom do, even during a player's unusually long "hot" streak. The shooter can ask for new dice at any time and his request will usually be honored.

If the shooter on the come-out roll throws a 2, 3, or 12, the results are a loss for the pass line bettors and a win for the don't pass wagers. A roll of 7 or 11 on the come-out is a win for those with their money on the pass line and loss for back-liners. A roll of 4, 5, 6, 8, 9 or 10 results in designation of a point, and the layout is marked with a puck to indicate the shooter's point.

After the designation of a point, the pass and don't pass line bets can no longer be changed because the point is in action. The shooter then tosses the dice until he tosses his point or a 7. Although there are many bets (the come, don't come and one-rollers) that can be made on each throw of the dice, the pass and don't pass line bets are only affected by the toss of the point number or a 7. If the point is thrown first, this is a winning roll and an amount equal to the pass line bet is paid by the dealer by placing it next to the initial wager. The shooter retains the dice and is free to change his bet in any manner he wishes, except that a minimum bet must be made to continue shooting. The next roll would be a new come-out roll. ,

If the shooter tosses a 7 before making his point, he sevens out (pass line bettors lose while back-liners win) and has to give up the dice. The player immediately to his left is then given the opportunity to shoot. Thus, when joining a casino game with several open positions, refrain from selecting one that would make you the next shooter. Common courtesy would dictate that you choose a spot in the general area to the right of the shooter. There is nothing more irritating to a player at the table than to have a new player squeeze in between him and the shooter just as he was about to be the next shooter.

Proposition, field, come and don't come bets, as previously stated, can be made at any time. The latter two bets are often confusing to the newcomer to Craps. Actually, the bet is made in the same manner as the pass line, by placing the wager in the come area, and the roll following the bet becomes the come-out roll for this wager. This bet can be made by anyone at the table, including a new arrival who otherwise would have to wait until there was a decision on the current point.

After making a bet on the come, you follow the same rules of Craps which apply to a come-out roll—the 2, 3, and 12 craps result in a loss, 7 and 11 naturals are a win. For a number 4, 5, 6, 8, 9, and 10 roll, this becomes the box number for this bet and is paid off as a winner if the particular number is tossed before a 7, and is lost if a 7 is tossed first. A come bet can be made on every roll except for the table come-out roll, at which the bet is made on the pass line. On the shooter's sevening out, the last come bet is a winner, since it is a "natural" for this bet.

When the dice are in play, make certain that your hands are kept away from the playing area. For the dice to strike a player's hands is often considered "bad" luck by many players, and to have the dice turn up an unfavorable 7 or craps at that time may result in a silent comment or two not exactly favorable to your personal well being.

Of course, if you are like most Craps players, your "big" moment comes when you are the shooter. Remember that a good Craps shooter will always toss the dice down the center of the table with enough force to strike the opposite backboard. This type of toss will minimize the possibility of hitting the dealers' hands, or of having the dice end up behind the dealer's supply of chips. While it may be a legal toss, your failure to hit the backboard with the dice is particularly irritating to some of the other players, especially on an unfavorable roll.

The Importance of Odds, Percentages, and Betting

Let us see how the odds and percentages of Craps are determined. First, there are 36 ways in which a pair of dice can come to rest, and in all cases the total will be some number from 2 to 12. The table below shows these eleven numbers and the number of possible combinations that form each number.

2 can be made in only one way: 1–1
3 can be made in two ways: 2–1, 1–2
4 can be made in three ways: 2–2, 3–1, 1–3
5 can be made in four ways: 2–3, 3–2, 4–1, 1–4
6 can be made in five ways: 5–1, 1–5, 4–2, 2–4, 3–3
7 can be made in six ways: 3–4, 4–3, 5–2, 2–5, 6–1, 1–6
8 can be made in five ways: 5–3, 3–5, 6–2, 2–6, 4–4
9 can be made in four ways: 6–3, 3–6, 5–4, 4–5
10 can be made in three ways: 6–4, 4–6, 5–5
11 can be made in two ways: 6–5, 5–6
12 can be made in one way: 6–6
Total: 36 Combinations

Knowing that there are thirty-six ways of making these eleven numbers and also how many ways each individual number can be made, it is not difficult to obtain the correct odds on all points and off-numbers. This is done simply by figuring the number of ways the *point* can be made as against the six combinations by which 7 can be made. The following chart gives the odds against passing or making the point. The correct odds are also shown in terms of money bets.

4 can be made in 3 ways, 7 in 6 ways—odds are 2 to 1 against the shooter
5 can be made in 4 ways, 7 in 6 ways—odds are 3 to 2 against the shooter
6 can be made in 5 ways, 7 in 6 ways—odds are 6 to 5 against the shooter
8 can be made in 5 ways, 7 in 6 ways—odds are 6 to 5 against the shooter
9 can be made in 4 ways, 7 in 6 ways—odds are 3 to 2 against the shooter
10 can be made in 3 ways, 7 in 6 ways—odds are 2 to 1 against the shooter

As was stated in Chapter 1, it is most important to know the odds. Actually, the major difference between the average player and an expert is the failure of non-professionals to take into account the actual odds on the various bets as opposed to the odds he receives from the house. Bets which pay off at much less than the correct odds are the quickest way to make a player's bankroll nose-dive. But, rather .than bore you with page after page of mathematical calculations, we have compiled the following table that gives you the essential information that you need to know about Craps' odds and percentages.

Bet	Chances Against		Chances For	House Pays	Percentage in House's Favor	House's Percentage on $5 Bet*
Pass Line	251	to	244	1 to 1	1.414	$.07
Come	251	to	244	1 to 1	1.414	.07
Don't Pass Bar 6–6	976	to	949	1 to 1	1.402	.07
Don't Come Bar 6–6	976	to	949	1 to 1	1.402	.07
Field (2, 3, 4, 9, 10, 11, 12)	20	to	16	1 to 1	11.111	.56
Field (2, 3, 4, 9, 10, 11, 12. Double on 2 or 12)	380	to	340	1 to 1	5.263	.26
Field (2, 3, 5, 9, 10, 11, 12)	19	to	17	1 to 1	5.555	.27
Big 6	6	to	5	1 to 1	9.090	.45
Big 8	6	to	5	1 to 1	9.090	.45
Any 7	5	to	1	4 to 1	16.666	.83
Any Craps	8	to	1	7 to 1	11.111	.56
Hard Way, 4 or 10	8	to	1	7 to 1	11.111	.56
Hard Way, 6 or 8	10	to	1	9 to 1	9.090	.45
11 or 3	17	to	1	14 to 1	16.666	.83
2 or 12	35	to	1	29 to 1	16.666	.83

* The Bank's edge on a $5 wager given in cents has, in each case a plus fraction which we have omitted.

From noting the percentages in the table, it is obvious that you should stay away from proposition and field bets. While they are *very* popular, they are *most* unprofitable for the player. Sometimes a so-called "high roller" will make a 7 or "any craps" bet as insurance against the come and pass line bets. A typical application of the any Craps insurance bet is as follows:

The bettor has $500 on the pass line and wants to assure not losing the bet in the case of any craps. He then places $75 on any craps. Should a craps come up, he would lose his pass line bet but be paid off $525 on the any craps bet, giving him a $25 profit plus the same bet on the pass line of $500, and on the previous any craps of $75. However, a knowledge of the mathematics of the game would show him that he is paying an 11.1 per cent premium on the $75 bet, or $8.20 for a single roll. By comparison the pass line bet of $500 has a house advantage of only $7, considering even the craps possibilities.

The same high roller often will insure himself against a 7 on a come-out roll when he has significant bets on the numbers via previous come wagers. Again, this is a poor bet because of the 16.7 per cent house advantage on the any 7 proposition.

Craps is not a game for the faint-hearted; there is no place for so-called insurance in the game. First, betting against yourself merely reduces the effective win possibility; and, secondly, the cost of this so-called insurance is so high as to be prohibitive.

Bets not on the Layout

There are several bets that are available to Craps players which do not appear on the table layout and are handled by the dealer or boxman. Some of them such as the "three-way craps" and "horn-bet" are one-roll sucker wagers that should be stayed away from. But, for the uninitiated, a "three-way craps" bet is a one-roll affair in which you are betting the same as "any craps," but in this case you are betting at least one chip on each of the crap numbers and your payoff, rather than being 7 to 1, is 14 to 1 if three is thrown and 29 to 1 if either 2 or 12 is rolled. In other words, three-way-craps is merely a simple way of telling the dealer you want a $1 bet on each of the three craps numbers. The house percentage on such a bet is 16.7 per cent.

The horn-bet is another 16.7 per cent house advantage wager. To place it, give the dealer four chips and call "horn-bet." This means that you are wagering one chip on each of the craps numbers plus 11. If 3 or 11 appears, you will be paid 14 to 1; if 2 or 12 comes up, the payoff is 29 to 1. This is a one roll bet and can be placed at any time.

Place Bets

The most popular of the non-layout wagers are the place bets and box numbers. On all layouts in Las Vegas, you will find the numbers 4, 5, 6, 8, 9, and 10 in boxes. These are called, "Place Numbers" or "Box Numbers." While these numbers are primarily for come-bets and don't-come bets (see page 29), they are used in many casinos for place bets. In most Las Vegas establishments, place wagers go on the line that separates the "do" and "don't" spaces for point numbers on the come and don't-come bets, or on the line in front of the numbered point box. Place bets can be made at any time and you do not have to wait for a new shooter.

To make a place bet, you merely hand your chips to the dealer and say "Place four," or "Place nine." You may call any number appearing in the boxes. This means you are betting that your number, in any combination, will appear before a 7. Here are the odds:

Point	Actual Odds	Correct Odds	Percentage in House's Favor	House's Percentage on $5 Bet
6 or 8	7 to 6	6 to 5	1.515	.08
5 or 9	7 to 5	7½ to 5	4.000	.20
4 or 10	9 to 5	10 to 5	6.666	.33

Be sure to memorize the "actual odds" figure because to get full advantage of them you must bet the exact amount to get the full payoff. For example, if you bet on 8, you must bet $6 for the house to pay off at $7. If you wagered $5, you would not be taking full advantage of the odds because, on a $5 bet, the odds would be a fraction of a dollar and casinos cannot take time to make such payoffs. That is, since the Strip casinos will not pay fractions of a dollar, you must make place bets on the numbers 4, 5, 9 or 10 in increments of five in order to have full advantage of the odds. If you bet on a 6 or 8, you should wager in units of six.

Many observers of a Craps game are confused when they see a player receive less than the amount he won. This is easily explained. The player wants to "press" his place bet, which means increasing it after a win. Therefore, when a player wins $9 on a $5 place bet on 4 or 10 and wants to "press" it, the dealer will put a $5 chip on top of the one already working and hand the player the $4 difference. The player now has a $10 place bet on which he may win $18.

When making bets that are off the craps table layout, the verbal wager is in play if it is repeated by the dealer. He will call "no bet" if in his judgment the bet call is too late for the roll in process. If the wager is accepted, you are expected to produce the chips necessary to cover the bet that you made. As a matter of fact, many craps table layouts have the words "no call bets accepted" on them. This refers, not so much to verbally announcing your bets or your intention of making them, which is sometimes necessary, but to calling out bets without producing the money or chips and letting go of it to signify that you are taking a risk. If you put more down on the table or hand more to the dealer than an announced bet actually requires, you will be paid off the proper amount for your win on the announced bet.

Buy Bets

Another way of wagering on a particular number in addition to place bets is the buying of a number. In buying a number the player pays an added 5 per cent commission on his bet of any of the box numbers (4, 5, 6, 8, 9, or 10) to obtain the correct odds on the number. This commission, which is charged against the short end of the bet and is payable at the time you make the bet, is called *vigorish* and, needless to say, is very helpful to the well-being of casino proprietors. You can see what we mean by looking at the following table:

Point	Buy Bet Odds Under 5% Commission	Percentage in House's Favor	House's Percentage on $5 Bet
4 or 10	2 to 1	4.761	.25
5 or 9	3 to 2	4.761	.25
6 or 8	6 to 5	4.761	.25

Buy bets, like the other place bets, are removable any time before a decision is reached on them. If you decide to drag down your bet, both the amount of the bet and the prepaid commission will be returned to you. The house earns that 5 per cent commission only when there is winning or losing action on your bet. To obtain full value from the commission, the short end of your bet should be for not less than twenty times the amount of the commission. Since the Strip casinos do not acknowledge fractions of a dollar, this means that lowest buy bet that can be effectively made in these establishments is $20 (5 per cent of $20 is $1; the $1 is the commission). If you are wagering large amounts the 5 per cent commission presents no special problem, but for the average player it makes a buy bet almost untouchable. But do not feel bad. Buy bets, if they are wagered, should be made only on the points 4 and 10. The regular place bets on 5, 6, 8 or 9 cost you less. Actually, the only buy or place bets that make any sense at all are *placing* the 6 or 8 which has a house advantage of 1.515 per cent. The other place or buy bets, which range from 4.000 to 6.666 per cent house advantage, are considered "sucker" or foolish wagers.

Incidentally, many Las Vegas casinos, at present, do not allow or else frown upon "placing" or "buying" back-line bets. In establishments which permit these "wrong" bets, you can see by the following table, that for the most part, they could be said to be sucker wagers that should be avoided.

Place Bets to Lose	Percentage in House's Favor	House's Percentage on $5 Bet
House takes 11 to 5 on 4 or 10*	3.030	.15
House takes 8 to 5 on 5 or 9	2.500	.12
House takes 5 to 4 on 6 or 8	1.818	.09

Buy Bets to Lose (5% Charge) *

House takes 2 to 1 on 4 or 10	2.439	.12
House takes 3 to 2 on 5 or 9	3.225	.16
House takes 6 to 5 on 6 or 8	4.000	.20

* This means that the house is taking the bet and is on the long end of the odds; you must thus put up eleven units to win the house's five.

Taking the Odds

This betting option, often called "free or full" odds, is seldom used by beginning Craps players and is rarely mentioned in any of the free literature distributed by the casinos. The reason for the latter is quite obvious; the house has no advantage at all in these bets since the odds are mathematically correct. That is, point 6 or 8 pays 6 to 5; point 5 or 9 pays 3 to 2; and point 4 or 10 pays 2 to 1. There is no marking on the craps table layout indicating how the taking of odds is possible. Here is how it is done:

When the shooter comes out on the point, practically all the Las Vegas casinos allow the players who have previously placed bets on the pass line to then make a second wager, usually equal to the flat or original bet, that the shooter will make his point. (Some Craps tables whose limit is $300 or $500 will allow only $150 or $250 respectively as a free maximum-limit odds bet, even though the front-line wager is greater.) If the point is made, the player receives even money for his original bet and the true odds on his secondary bet.

As with the place bet, it is important to memorize the free odds so that you receive the exact amount of your payoff. For instance, the 5 and 9 should be in increments of two so that the wager can be paid at 3 to 2. The 4 and 10 may be wagered in increments of one so the house pays 2 to 1. The 6 and 8 should be in increments of five, so that the bettor can be paid 6 to 5. In the latter case, you cannot take the odds for a flat bet of $1 or $2, but most casinos will allow you to make a $5 odds bet for a $3 or $4 flat bet.

To illustrate a wager when taking the odds, let us suppose a shooter rolls a 9 for his point. If you have made a bet of $5 on the pass line, you may take the odds with a wager of $2, $4 or $6. The procedure is to set the free odds bet in back of the pass line wager and call out to the dealer that you are taking the odds. If the shooter makes his point, you will receive even money for your pass line wager and 1½ times the full odds wager. (The point 9 pays the true odds of 3 to 2.) In other words, to take the odds, you must first place a flat bet on the pass line. Then, after the come-out toss in which the point is established, you have the option of making a second bet at the true odds. If the shooter sevens out you lose both bets. If he makes his point, you win both bets.

In most casinos you can also take full odds on flat come bets *after* your come number has been established. Taking the odds on a come number is made by placing the amount of the odds bet before the dealer after a particular come roll on which you have made a flat come bet and stating "odds" or "full odds." He will then place your come bet on the come number with the odds wager somewhat displaced to indicate that this portion of your bet should be paid off at full odds. Remember to be patient with the dealer when taking the odds, but do not be timid about attracting his attention. There may be other players competing for his attention, too. The dealer is not a mind reader and he will welcome your telling him what the money is for when you hand it to him.

On paying off a winning roll on a previous bet, the dealer will generally put the original come bet and odds wager in the come area. Your payoff for your flat come bet will be placed next to the come wager and the full odds payoff will be found next to the odds bet, with the bonus portion easily noted.

There is a *general* house policy in most of Vegas' casinos that all odds bets (including place and buy wagers) are "off" on the come-out toss. You can, if you wish, have your free odds bets in play even on the come-out by stating to the dealer that your wager is "on" or "working." Since there is no mathematical advantage or disadvantage either way, the decision as to whether the odds bet is "on" or "off" on the come-out roll is a matter of personal preference. Remember that you are free to change your mind at any time and call the odds off, reduce the size of the free odds wager, or remove it completely. Since there is no house advantage to these bets, the casinos are not particularly anxious for you to take the odds.

Taking the odds, as was stated previously, is restricted to

players who have flat bets. Very rarely an exception may be made in the case of one player staking another (furnishing the money for his gambling) or perhaps a husband and wife, playing at the same table, who may be considered as one for betting purposes. Under the circumstances, for example, the husband could take the odds in connection with his wife's line bet if she neglected to do so herself. If there are relatively few players at a table and the dealer gives his consent to this, it is all right. Do not, however, attempt it or even ask to do it at a very busy table, because the dealers have enough to do and think about already without becoming involved in attempting to remember who is wagering for someone else.

As we have said many times in this book—and it cannot be over-emphasized—the only way to gamble effectively is to keep the house advantage to a minimum. This can best be accomplished by limiting your bets to the pass line and come spaces only and always taking the free odds. Under the free odds condition, the house edge falls to 0.848 per cent—by far the best regular bet in the entire casino. At one time a few casinos in Las Vegas allowed you to take "double" free odds which lowered the house advantage to 0.606 per cent. The term "double odds" refers to the allowance of free odds bet of twice the magnitude of the associated flat wager. Unfortunately, for the gambler, double odds are a thing of the past in Las Vegas. But, in any case, keep Sam Landy's fine advice in mind: "Always take the odds . . . even if you go broke."

Laying the odds

If you are a back-line bettor, you must lay odds instead of taking odds. In this case, you are wagering that the point will not be made, since you are betting against the dice. If the shooter sevens out, you will be appropriately paid at 1 to 2, 2 to 3, or 5 to 6, depending on what the point is.

It is important again, of course, to make your bets in the correct increments. That is, the wager should be in increment of six for the 6 and 8 to pay 5 for 6. For the 4 and 10, the bet should be in increments of two to pay 1 for 2. For 5 and 9, the wager should be in increment of three to be paid 2 for 3. In most casinos that permit laying odds it is usually possible to make larger bets on the odds than what you have on the back line, larger in an amount such that, if you win, the payoff to you equals your flat or original wrong bets.

Let us suppose you have placed a $5 bet on the don't pass section and the shooter throws 10. In casinos where you are permitted to lay odds, you may place an additional bet outside the layout behind the don't pass line. Since the shooter threw a 10 in our example, you must bet in increments of two, up to $10. If the shooter sevens out before he makes a 10, you receive even money for the lnie wager and one-half the odds bet. That is, if you lay the odds of $10, you would receive even money for your original $5 wager and another $5 for the $10 you laid.

The back-line bettor enjoys an equally low percentage bet (0.832 per cent). For this reason, if you bet the don't pass line or don't come, it is always wise to lay the odds.

In closing this chapter on Craps, it is safe to say that the best buys in the game are the pass, come, don't pass, don't come bets and to take or lay the full free odds. Playing these bets and the avoidance of all proposition bets is by far the best way to play, and is the mark of an expert player. Playing in such a manner, even at low betting levels, coupled with proper money management, makes you an intelligent player and more dangerous to the casino than the "high rollers." Do not be intimidated by the action of these players; most of them do not know how to play the game properly. The amount of money you wager does not make you a better or worse player; the technique of your play determines your classification. This may be hard to believe, but it can be vouched for by the casino management personnel as being completely true.

3

♠

Blackjack, or Twenty-One

"Hit me and make it good" is the cry as one to six people play to beat the dealer and woo fickle fate. Of the thousands of card games, Blackjack, or Twenty-One, as it is more correctly known, is one of the easiest to understand and perhaps the most exciting to play. It is usually considered the second-best gambling buy for the "average" player in Las Vegas.

The Basic Elements of the Game

The first step in mastering Blackjack—or any game, for that matter—is a thorough understanding of the rules governing its play. While many people have played Blackjack at home with their friends where "home rules" have applied, the average person on his first visit to a Las Vegas casino is generally somewhat bewildered by the rules. In addition to this, confusion is often heightened by the fact that Blackjack rules vary slightly from casino to casino. Thus it is always a good idea to check with the dealer regarding interpretation of house rules before starting play. As to the play itself, here are the basic essentials:

Layout

Blackjack is played on a semi-circular table covered with green felt. During the course of play, the dealer stands behind the table

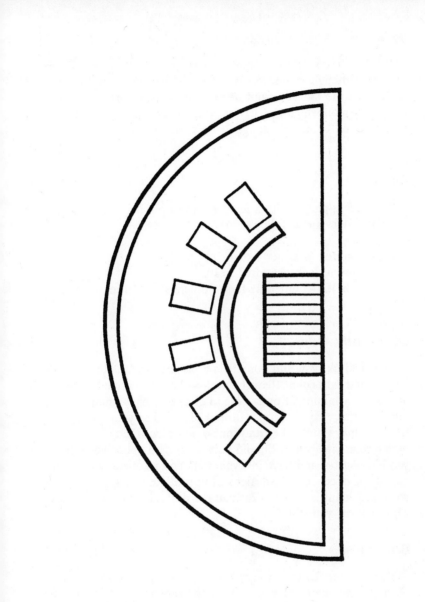

Blackjack table layout.

while the players sit opposite him. There are usually spaces for six players, although a few casinos employ five and others seven spaces. On the table in front of each player is a square, circle, or other design on which the players place their wagers. All bets must be placed on or in this designated area before the start of *each* deal.

Cards

Blackjack is played with a regular deck of playing cards in which the card values are as follows:

Ace—counted as either 1 or 11.
King, Queen, Jack—counted as 10.
2 through 10—counted at their numerical identities, or at face value.

Object of the Game

In Blackjack, you and your fellow players attempt to obtain a higher total card count than the dealer—he is considered to be the house—by attaining 21 or as close to 21 as possible without exceeding that sum. At your proper turn of play and at your own discretion, you may stand pat or draw one or more cards in an attempt to better your card count. Should your total card count go over 21, you have *busted* and have lost your bet. You must turn your cards face up at once, and the dealer will immediately pick them up. If your card count is closer to 21 than the dealer or should he exceed 21, of course, you win.

Betting Limits

You must make your wager before receiving your first card by placing the amount of your bet on the spot reserved for it. The casino places both a minimum and maximum limit on what you can bet. On the Las Vegas Strip, the minimum bet limit is usually $1, while the maximum ranges from $100 to $500. There are times, especially when high rollers, or big spenders, are present, that the house will raise the maximum to $1,000. If you like your Blackjack action small and cannot stand the $1 minimum, chances are good that a game with a minimum as low as 25 cents may be found in downtown Vegas. Information pertaining to the limits is supposed to be posted at the table or on a sign prominently displayed close to it, but a few casinos are somewhat delinquent in publicizing this important information.

Methods of Dealing

While one to four standard fifty-two-card decks may be employed in the game, a single deck is still the common practice in most Las Vegas casinos. The use of double and multi-decks result in a slightly higher house percentage and their use has been threatened by the casino owners for some time.

Before play begins, the dealer shuffles the cards and places them in front of the player whose turn it is to cut. The cut is usually made by inserting a Joker face up into the deck at any place he chooses and the dealer completes the cut at that point. Some casinos permit the standard cutting procedure used in most card games. But whatever method of cutting is employed, the deck's top card is "burned," or placed face up against the bottom of the pack. In most casinos, the dealer never looks at the burned card, nor does he show it to the players. However, if you wish to know the card, it is permissible to ask. It is optional with the dealer whether or not he will reveal the burned card. Most pit bosses stand behind their dealer's decision on this matter.

A single deck is either held in the dealer's hand or laid on the table layout as the cards are being dealt out. While it is customary for the dealer to pick up the "used" cards at the end of each hand of play and place them below the burned card, a few casinos now have their dealers stack the used cards face down on a designated place on the layout. Where this method is employed, it is not necessary to burn a card and thus the full fifty-two cards may be used. For when the top card is burned the last card in the deck cannot be used either and the play of the game is confined to only the fifty cards in-between. That is, when, during play, the dealer reaches the card ahead of the burned card, he re-shuffles the cards in his hand and offers them to a player to cut, again burning a card before restarting play. Incidentally, with either method, the dealer has the option to shuffle the cards at any time between hands.

Where two or more decks are employed, an open-faced box, or *shoe*, is used to hold the cards. This dealing box remains on the table and cards are withdrawn from it one at a time by the dealer. The used cards can either be placed in back of the movable partition in the shoe or stacked face down on layout, depending on how the casino prefers this detail to be handled. A burned card is generally used to mark the need for a shuffle. Actually, the shoe is now being used in a few casinos even for a single deck and there has been some talk that Nevada Gaming Commission *may* require a dealing box to be used on all games of Blackjack in the state.

At present there is a difference as to how single and multi-decks are dealt. In the case of the former, the first two cards given to the players are delivered face down, while those dealt from multi-deck shoe are generally turned face up. (In some of the casinos on the Strip where multi-decks are employed, the cards are dealt in the same manner as a single deck.) Under either arrangement, the dealer's first two cards are dealt one face up and second face down. All additional cards to either the players or dealer are dealt face up.

The Play of the Game

Once the cards are dealt, the dealer offers each player the option of staying pat with the first two cards or drawing more. There are, however, two exceptions to this basic procedure:

1. If the dealer's face-up, or showing, card is an Ace or a 10-value card, he will look at his down, or hole, card without revealing it to the players. Should the dealer have a *natural* 21 (Ace and 10-value card), or Blackjack, he will turn over his down card and will collect all bets except those by players who have Blackjack and standoff, or tie, him.

2. If the dealer's showing card is an Ace, he will offer "insurance" to each of the players prior to looking at his hole card. This gives each player the opportunity to insure his hand against the possibility of dealer having a natural 21. That is, any player wish-

ing to insure his bet against the dealer having Blackjack must place one-half his original bet in the betting area directly in front of him. When all players have had the chance to make an insurance bet, the dealer then looks at his hole card. If it is a 10-value card, giving him a natural, he then pays all players who made insurance bets 2 to 1 on the amount of their insurance bet and then takes the amount of their original bet. If, however, the dealer does not have Blackjack he collects the amount of the insurance bets only. The advantages and disadvantages of insuring a bet will be discussed later in this chapter.

When the dealer does not hold Blackjack, the player at his extreme left plays first. If the player holds a natural 21, he calls Blackjack and turns his cards up so the dealer can verify the count. The dealer then pays off the player at 3 to 2 odds, or 1½ times the money he has bet. If the player's two cards total less than 21 he may decide:

1. *To stand pat.* He has reached this decision because he is satisfied with his count or fears that a third card may "bust" his hand by making his card total go over 21. He simply says "I stand," "Good," or "I'm O.K." He may also signify that he is standing pat by sliding his cards under the chips he has bet.

2. *To draw one or more additional cards.* This decision is usually reached because the player is not satisfied with the card count. In such a case, he says, "Hit me," or makes a come-on motion with his finger or by scratching the table with his cards. The dealer then gives the player a card off the top of the deck face up and next to his original two cards. If a player wants a fourth, fifth or sixth card he may have it. Thus, when he feels that his count is as good as he can get, he says "I have enough," or makes a stop sign. But, should he go over 21, he must turn his down cards face up immediately and surrender his bet.

The play moves to the player's left, clockwise around the table until each player either stands or busts. If a player should forget to hit a hand he may *not* ask to be hit after the dealer has dealt to the next player. If a down card is accidentally exposed during play, it does *not* invalidate a hand.

In casino Twenty-One, the dealer *always* plays last. Should all players bust, he merely places his own cards face up on the bottom deck (or the designated place on the layout), and deals the next round. If any *active* players remain in the game, the dealer must play his hand as follows:

1. He turns his hole card up, exposing all his cards.

2. If his total count is 16 or less, the dealer must draw a card. He must keep drawing cards until his total is 17 or more.

3. If the dealer's count is 17 or more, he must *stand*—in most major casinos—even if he has a soft 17 (meaning a 17 count using an Ace as 11, plus a six spot). There are still a few clubs in Las Vegas that require a dealer to *hit* on a soft 17. This vital information is usually printed right on the table layout. But, if it is not, be sure to check with the dealer before starting play. It is to the advantage of the player for the dealer to stand on a soft 17.

4. Once the dealer stands, he pays even money for their bets to those players with higher totals than his and collects the bets of those who have a lower count. Ties, or "pushes," between players and dealer are standoffs, with no money changing hands. If the dealer busts, he must pay off at even money to all the players still in the game. But, in any case, the active players should not turn over their cards; this is the task of the dealer. After he flips over the players' cards and verifies the count, the payoff is made.

As you can see, the Blackjack dealer has no choice of action. His decisions as to whether he stays pat or draws are predetermined and are known to the players before play starts. Since all his cards are exposed at his turn of play, the dealer has no opportunity for any departure from the house rules.

Play for the next hand starts almost immediately. That is, for the players wishing to play, bets are made and the deal begun *generally* without re-shuffling the cards. As described earlier, the dealer continues from where the play was interrupted by exhaustion of the cards in his hand or in the shoe. At this point, the dealer shuffles the cards, even in the midst of the play of a hand. Also as previously stated, the dealer has the right to shuffle at *any time* between hands. The player may also request a shuffle between hands. Some dealers comply, while others may refuse. In addition, the player by custom, but not required by house rules, is able to request a new deck whenever he desires. When a new deck is introduced in a game, it is generally spread out face down. This permits the dealer to inspect the backs of the cards for any imperfections that could be used by the players to identify cards when they are face down. Then the cards are spread face up. This gives the players an opportunity to make sure that no cards have been added to or removed from the deck. The dealer can put a new deck into play at any time according to his own discretion.

Betting Options

There are two very important betting options that a player must always consider. They are:

Splitting. If a player is dealt two cards of identical value, he has the option of "splitting" the pair and playing each card as a separate hand. This is done by turning up his cards and by doubling his original wager to cover his twin hands. The dealer then gives him a second card face down on each hand. From this point on, he plays each hand separately, standing or drawing in the normal manner—with several minor exceptions.

First, if a player splits a pair and draws a third card of identical value to the first two, most casinos permit him to split again to form a third hand. The same procedure as described above must be followed.

Another exception is that if a natural 21 results from a split pair the player is paid off at only even money.

And finally, should a player receive a pair of Aces and split them, he receives one card—and only one card—on each Ace. If a split Ace is hit with another Ace, the house rules in most casinos will not allow the player to split for a third time. Again, if a natural should occur, the hand is not considered a Blackjack, but simply a 21.

Doubling Down. While the rules for "doubling down" vary in Las Vegas, most casinos will allow a player to double on any two cards. After the first two cards are dealt, a player, wishing to double down, turns his cards face up and informs the dealer that he desires to double the bet—then doubles his bet. (Incidentally, some casinos do not require an exact doubling of the bet and will permit the adding of any amount up to the original wager.) After the additional wager has been added to the original bet, the dealer gives the player *only* one card face down. The total of the three cards now represents the player's hand—no more cards may be drawn. The correct occasions to double down, as well as when to split pairs, will be explained later in this chapter.

These are the basic elements of Blackjack play. Let us now take a look at finer techniques as viewed by our Las Vegas experts, under the direct co-ordination of Sherlock Feldman, well-known pit boss at the Dunes Hotel.

Blackjack Strategy

Unlike the other casino games, Blackjack was not originally devised with specified odds against the player. It evolved from a home-type card game and was adapted to casino play. For this reason, it is rather difficult to give *exact* house advantage percentage as with the other casino games. Actually, with each card dealt the house percentage varies ever so slightly. But most experts agree that the house percentage against a *good* player is from 2 to 3 per cent. The *smart* player who takes full advantage of all play factors, however, can shave this percentage to *almost* zero. Actually, some mathematicians and gaming theoreticians claim that the house's advantage is *less* than 0.2 per cent when Blackjack is played with computer accuracy. Actually, Blackjack is about the only casino game in which skill plays any part. Let us take a look at some of the advantages that the player has:

1. The player is paid at odds of 3 to 2 when he holds a natural 21.

2. Unlike the dealer, the player can stand or hit on any card count provided he does not exceed 21. That is, at his turn of play he may draw or stand pat.

3. The player is the one who determines the amount of the wager and can increase or lower it as he sees fit within the prescribed casino betting limits.

4. The player may split pairs or double down if the situation appears favorable.

5. In some casinos, the player may play as many hands as there are available betting spaces.

6. The player may count, or "case," the deck. By remembering the cards previously played and exposed, his chances of winning are a great deal better. An expert card-counter once profited by more than $25,000 at a downtown Las Vegas casino because the establishment's boss stubbornly refused to believe that card casing would give a player any degree of an advantage.

7. The player has the opportunity to see one of the dealer's cards and may use this information in determining the play of his hand.

8. The dealer is not interested in the cards the players are holding, since the rule by which he plays—drawing to 16 and standing on all 17—is inflexible. Up until recently, it was thought that this prohibition on the dealer gave the house an advantage in that it relieved the dealer of making individual decisions that could work to the house's disadvantage. Now, electronic computer studies show that this premise may not be completely true. As a matter of fact, the house's only real advantage is that *the dealer plays last.* If it were not for this rule, the player's chances of winning would be as good—maybe better—than the dealer's. The player often will start out with a hand that is potentially better than the dealer's—but if he busts (goes over 21) with it the house collects on the bet it might otherwise have lost. It is also because of this rule that the player who follows the dealer's procedure of hitting all totals to 16 and standing on 17 and higher is doomed to failure. A player that does so incurs a disadvantage of about 6 per cent and this is too high for successful play.

To be a "smart," or educated, Blackjack player you must:

1. Know the basic elements of the game, especially when to hit or stand, and whether or not to split pairs or double down.

2. Case or count the cards that have been drawn from the deck, and which cards have not been played from the pack. This is much more difficult than in other card games such as Bridge and Pinochle since in Blackjack there is no set fashion in which the cards will fall.

3. Know money management—when to wager big and when to bet small.

The Strategy for Hitting and Standing

The only players who win consistently at Blackjack over the long run are those who draw to beat the dealer. All too many players beat themselves by drawing improperly. That is, they take chances which invariably make them bust. The educated player, on the other hand, utilizes the dealer's two major disadvantages—his one card exposed and the house rule's determining his play. For instance, when the dealer's exposed card indicates there is a good chance that he will have to draw and may go bust, the smart player will play so that the chances are that he will not. Thus, the first step in learning to become an "expert" Blackjack player is to know when to stand and when to hit.

For this information, we have tabulated the advice given by the dealers and pit bosses of several major casinos and then compared it to the findings of two computer tests. The results are as follows:

If you have 17 or more, regardless of what the dealer shows, stand pat—do not hit. All too often players with 17 forget this strategy when the dealer's up card is 10, Jack, Queen or King. They are sure that he has a 10-value card in the hole. Thus they will hit and go over. Remember that it is not an easy matter to have a pat hand of from 17 to 20. The chances are less than 1 in 3.

There are three exceptions to this basic rule of standing on 17—all of them have to do with doubling down and splitting. For instance, it is wise to split a pair of 9's, except when the dealer shows a 7, 10 or Ace. Likewise, it is considered good play to double down on a *soft* 17 (Ace-6) when the dealer shows 3, 4, 5, or 6, and hit when 2, 7, 8, 9, 10, or Ace are exposed. Likewise, on a *soft* 18, it is wise to stand if dealer shows 2, 3, 7, 8 or Ace; double down on 4, 5, 6; or hit on a 9 or 10.

If you have 13 thru 16 and the dealer shows 2, 3, 4, 5, or 6, stand pat—do not hit. Any time a player receives a card count of 13 to 16, he is considered to be holding a "stiff," or bad, hand. It is most important in such instances to capitalize on the dealer's inflexible play. For example, let us suppose that the dealer's up card is a 6 and you are holding 13. The dealer's chances of making a count of 17 to 21 are less than 1 to 2, but your hopes of drawing a card which will give you 17 to 21 are even less than that—approximately 2 to 5. It is always better to let the dealer run the risk of busting.

If you have 13 thru 16 and the dealer shows 7 or more, hit. Here is where some of the experts disagreed. While they said that they would hit 14 or 15, about half said no to 16. But when we checked the computer figures, it showed that the chances of the player hitting and busting were about 3 out of 5. It also indicated that if the player did not hit, the dealer's chances of winning were greater than that—3½ out of 5. Thus, it is wise to hit a stiff hand until you have a 17 or better when the dealer shows 7 or higher.

The strategy for soft 13 thru 16 is given on page 73.

If you have 12 and the dealer shows 4 thru 6, stand pat—do not hit. This is another stiff hand that can cause problems for a player. While you can probably think of dozens and dozens of combinations that will permit you to reach 17 to 21 when you have 12, remember they are outnumbered by all the cards which can send you over 21. Of course, do not be afraid to hit this stiff hand if the dealer's up card is 2, 3, 7 or more. As you will see later in this chapter, card casing or counting can be a great help in deciding the play of a stiff hand.

If you have 11, regardless of what the dealer shows, double down. This strategy may cause some consternation among professional Twenty-One gamblers. Until computers came along the general strategy was never to double down on 11 when the dealer had 9, 10, or Ace showing. But now it has proven best to always double down on a card total of 11, double on a total 10 unless the dealer's up-card is 10 or Ace, and double on a total of 9 when the dealer shows 7 or higher. The edge in favor of doubling becomes successively smaller for 10 and 9, and it is not usually advisable to double on 8 or lower. (The computer indicates a *slight* player advantage in doubling down on 8 when dealer shows either a 5 or 6, but most experts frown on this bit of electronic advice and we will go along with them only as a matter of simplicity.) There are numerous instances, however, that will tempt the more adventurous gambler who does not mind bucking a percentage against him if that percentage is not too high. The expert who is accurately casing the deck goes by the actual situation, not by published guides. If he sees that only low cards remain in the deal, he would prefer to play his hand straight and draw as many cards as he wants rather than double down to get stuck with a low final count. Remember that doubling the bet means you can draw only one additional card and if it should be a low one, you have no chance unless the dealer busts. Several casinos in Las Vegas will permit doubling *only* on 10 and 11, so be sure of the house rules before you start play.

How to handle 10 and below. As previously mentioned, it is sometimes wise to double down on 10 and 9. Except for doubling down as noted, it is necessary, of course, to hit low card count until they are raised to at least 12. From then on, follow the advice given earlier for plays of 12, 13 thru 16, and 17 and more.

FREQUENCY OF PLAYING NUMBERS

No.	Ways of Making	No.	Ways of Making
16	23,020	19	72,380
17	37,970	20	102,120
18	51,700	21	171,060

MAKING PLAYING NUMBER WITH 2 CARDS

No.	Ways of Making	No.	Ways of Making
16	102	19	80
17	96	20	136
18	86	21	64

Odds on making 21 with 2 cards	24–1
Odds on getting 16 or better with 2 cards	1.5–1

MAKING PLAYING NUMBER WITH 3 CARDS

No.	Ways of Making	No.	Ways of Making
16	1,344	19	1,680
17	1,488	20	1,894
18	1,580	21	2,052

Odds on making 21 with 3 cards	13.3–1
Odds on getting 16 or better with 3 cards	1.9–1
Odds on overdrawing with 3 cards	2–1

MAKING PLAYING NUMBER WITH 4 CARDS

No.	Ways of Making	No.	Ways of Making
16	5,055	19	9,744
17	6,240	20	11,297
18	7,650	21	12,420

Odds on making 21 with 4 cards	19–1
Odds on getting 16 or better with 4 cards	4.3–1
Odds on overdrawing with 4 cards	1–2

Splitting pairs. There are favorable and unfavorable pair-splitting situations in Twenty-One. For instance it is never smart play to split 10-count cards. A 20 is fairly difficult to obtain in two cards. As you can see in the frequency of playing numbers chart, there are 136 two-card combinations to make 20. The odds are a little over 8½ to 1 against your having 20 with two cards. Not so easy to get 20, is it? The odds against you to have a pair of 5s or 4s are much larger. These are good hands, so why split them? (The only exception to this, according to the computer, is in the case of 4s when the dealer shows a 5. The odds in this instance *slightly* favor splitting.)

There are pairs that should be split, but experts often disagree as to which ones. For instance, one group says always split a pair of 8s, while others contend it best to split them only against a dealer's 2 through 7. The latter group reasons that when you have a pair of 8s and the dealer has 8, 9, 10 or Ace up, you have a bad hand and should just hit your 16. It is a bad hand and you can make it into a good hand. If you should lose it, you are only losing one bet instead of two by splitting.

There are counts that all experts agree on. Aces, for instance, should always be split. There are also cases where there is little doubt about the benefits derived from splitting. As a case in point, 7s are a good split against the dealer's 2 through 8 showing, because 14 is a bad hand and there are thirty-two cards to improve it. For example, you can catch one of sixteen pictures, which will give you 17, one of four Aces which will give you 18, a 2, 3 or 4 which will give you 9, 10, or 11 which will give you a chance to draw a high card for a winning hand. The same reasoning holds good for 6s, except in this case the split should be made only against the dealer's 2 through 7.

Split 2s and 3s when the dealer's up-card is 2, 3, 4, 5, 6 or 7.

Because of the human element of our experts, we will go along with the computer results for splitting given above. But, remember when you have a pair and the chart does not call for a split, just hit the pair and play the hand the way the chart says.

Soft hand play. "Soft" totals and what to do with them usually present some of the most difficult problems for a novice player. Actually, the only thing to remember in playing a soft hand is that the Ace may be counted as 1 or 11 and adjust your card count accordingly. For example, the dealer's up card is a 3, the player hits a soft 15 and draws an 8. His total count is now 13. If he counted the Ace as 11, he would be bust at 23. Thus his hand can no longer be considered "soft" and the player must revert to his standard strategy and stand on a "hard" 13. Any hand not counting an Ace as 11 is called a *hard* hand.

The strategy for hitting, standing, doubling down and splitting just discussed has been summarized in the following table. Committing it to memory is the first step in becoming an educated Blackjack player. Keep in mind, though, "Lady Luck" calls the final turn.

Your Cards	Dealer's Up Card	Your Action
17 or above	All	Stand
13 thru 16	2,3,4,5,6	Stand
	7,8,9,10,Ace	Hit
12	2,3,7,8,9,10,Ace	Hit
	4,5,6	Stand
11	All	Double Down
10	2,3,4,5,6,7,8,9	Double Down
	10,Ace	Hit
9	2,3,4,5,6	Double Down
	7,8,9,10,Ace	Hit
8 or less	All	Hit
Ace, Ace	All	Split
10,10	All	Stand
9,9	2,3,4,5,6,8,9	Split
	7,10,Ace	Stand
8,8	All	Split
7,7	2,3,4,5,6,7,8	Split
	9,10,Ace	Hit
6,6	2,3,4,5,6,7	Split
	8,9,10,Ace	Hit
5,5	All	Hit
4,4	2,3,4,6,7,8,9,10,Ace	Hit
	5	Split
3,3 and 2,2	2,3,4,5,6,7	Split
	8,9,10,Ace	Hit
Ace, 8 or 9	All	Stand
Ace, 7	2,3,7,8,Ace	Stand
	4,5,6	Double Down *
	9,10	Hit

Your Cards	Dealer's Up Card	Your Action
Ace, 6	2,7,8,9,10,Ace	Hit
	3,4,5,6	Double Down **
Ace, 3 thru 5	2,3,7,8,9,10,Ace	Hit
	4,5,6	Double Down **
Ace, 2	2,3,4,7,8,9,10,Ace	Hit
	5,6	Double Down **

* If doubling down is not permitted by house rules, stand.
** If doubling down is not permitted by house rules, hit.

Insurance Bet. The insurance bet, where it is offered, means that the house is willing to lay 2 to 1 when the dealer is showing an Ace that the dealer will *not* have a natural 21. Your bet, from the player's standpoint, is that the dealer *will* get a Blackjack. This is a *poor* bet under most circumstances.

Many old-time Las Vegas "experts" will tell you that when the dealer shows an Ace and you hold a natural, take out insurance. They contend that this is the only time when it pays you to take out insurance, for by doing so you *make certain of winning*. Let us make a mathematical analysis of this statement:

First, let us see what happens if you take out insurance. Assuming that your original bet is $2, this means that you must put up $1 for insurance. Now, if the dealer has a natural, you tie on your own Blackjack, and win $2 on the insurance bet. If the dealer does not have a natural, you win $3 on your Blackjack, but lose your $1 insurance. In either case, your profit is $2.

Now, if you do not take out insurance and the dealer has Blackjack, you have a standoff, which means your profit is zero. But, if he does not have it, your gain is $3. At first blush, it may appear that insurance, when you have a natural, is a good deal. True, the player who insures his Blackjack has about the only *safe* bet in gambling. But computer studies reveal that *less* than ⅓ of the time will both the player and dealer tie. In other words, *more* than ⅔ of the time, the player has the possibility of gaining 1½ to 1. While the old-timers are completely correct in their statement that you are certain to win when insuring your natural, you never receive its *full* value since you are paying off a house advantage of about 8 per cent to insure this win. As a matter of fact, the only players who make good use of insurance bets are those who can case the deck. Say, for example, the dealer shows an Ace and you know that out of twelve cards left in the deck six of them are 10-value cards. In this case, the odds that the dealer will get Blackjack are 1 to 1, but the odds the insurance bet offers you are 2 to 1. By all means, it is wise to take the bet under such circumstances.

Casing the Deck

One of the most valuable adjuncts that any Twenty-One player can have is the faculty of remembering most of the previously exposed cards. The player who does not develop this aptitude to some degree has little chance of beating the house in the long run, no matter how well he plays otherwise. Because the house's favorable advantage varies with the dealing of each card, the smart player also changes his strategy accordingly. The more dealt cards the player can remember, the greater chance he has of making the proper decisions on future hands.

Counting, or casing, the deck has been going on for years, but in recent years such gaming theoreticians as Dr. Allan Wilson, Roger Baldwin, and Dr. Edward Thorp have publicized the fact that this is the only way to beat Blackjack. Unfortunately, most of their methods, while very well-founded, are too complicated and require memorization beyond the range of the average player. In addition, many of their theories are based on a one-player-vs.-dealer situation. In Las Vegas such playing conditions are seldom possible.

You do not have to have a photographic memory or other great skill to be fairly successful in casing the deck. In this book, we are not going to cover any of the expert casing methods, but rather give you a few fundamentals that will help to develop your own method.

If you can keep track of the 10-count cards and Aces, for example, this information will be most beneficial for the double down plays, insurance bets, and for knowing the chances for busting. Remember that one-third of the deck, minus the Aces, are 10-counters. That is, one out of every three cards should be a 10. But, rather than counting the 10s as they are played, devise a method of keeping a running proportion of the number still in the deck. Here is one method that is quite popular in Las Vegas.

Essentially this method of simple casing involves the proportion number of 10s in each hand. When no 10s show in the player's hand, the count is one plus—which indicates that there is one extra 10 left in the deck in proportion to the remainder of the deck. (Remember that the *average* Blackjack hand contains three cards and there are sixteen 10-counters in a deck.) Should there be two 10 counters in a hand, the score is one minus—the one minus indicating that one less 10 remains in proportion to the remainder of the deck. As each hand is turned up, a mental running count is made. A separate mental note is also made of the Aces, but is not included with the 10s. Here are several Blackjack hands that will show how the running count is made:

K, 2, 7 (even)
3, 7, 2, 4 (1 plus)
9, 4, 6 (2 plus)
K, Q (1 plus)
5, A, Q (1 Ace and 1 plus)
10, 2, 10 (even)
7, 4, 5 (1 plus)
K, A (2 Aces and 1 plus)
4, Q, J (even)
J, 3, K (1 minus)
9, 4, 6 (even)
8, 4, A, 9 (3 Aces and 1 plus)

In the first hand, there was a 10-value card (the King); therefore, the running count was even. In the next hand, there were no 10s, so a one plus means an overbalance of 10s in the deck. (An overbalanced deck is often said to be a positive deck, while an underbalanced one is a negative deck.) The following hand had no 10s either, thus there was an overbalance of two plus. The player's 20 in the next hand shows one extra 10 which brings the count to one plus. In the next hand, the Ace is considered separately, while the one 10 leaves the overbalance the same. When the deck is highly positive or the overbalance is high and Ace count low, this is considered the ideal condition for the player because there are more 10s and Aces in proportion left in the deck. This means the chances for a natural 21 are greater. When the deck is highly negative or underbalance is high, it is usually a safe bet to hit a stiff hand.

To become proficient in the proportion count method of card casing, some practice is required. With a standard deck of cards, turn one card over at a time and keep a running count. The casing should end up with an even count, plus four Aces. Once you can go through the deck rapidly without any difficulty, have someone act as a dealer and practice casing the 10s and Aces in actual Blackjack hands. At first, start with two hands (the dealer's and yours). As your counting technique improves, increase the number of hands until you are able to cope with seven (the dealer's and six players'). Learn to spot the 10 count and Aces quickly, since in a casino game the dealer scoops up the cards rapidly.

Continue your practice as near as possible under game conditions. Sometimes, for instance, the cards will all be dealt out before the round has been completed. In such cases, the dealer shuffles the discards and continues dealing. When this occurs, the card count reverts to even 10s and zero Aces. Then recase all exposed cards and start your normal count. But be sure, when the dealer shuffles, to say to yourself, "Even 10s and zero Aces," otherwise the change is easily missed.

With just a little practice, you will be surprised at how proficient you can become in casing 10s and Aces. While this simple method is usually sufficient for the average player, you may wish to expand your casing prowess further. If you do, we suggest reading a book that contains advance techniques. For instance, Donald I. Collver's *Scientific Blackjack* (Arco Publishing Company) describes a procedure fairly similar to the one just described. However, it carries the system further to casing all the cards in the deck. Of course, the ultimate of all card casing methods is detailed in Dr. Thorp's book, *Beat the Dealer*, but it is far too complicated for the occasional Blackjack player. Also, some of his theories and claims are questioned by many of Las Vegas' Blackjack "experts."

A good card caser will always try to locate himself in the seat at the dealer's extreme right—called by the experts "third base"—because it is the best vantage point for keeping track of the exposed cards. Let us say, for instance, that he has a stiff hand with a count 13 after some 32 cards have been played. Of these 32 cards, he observes that fourteen were 10-value ones and three were 9s. With this information in mind, he knows that there are only three cards left in the deck that can bust him, so he will hit a hand that might normally call for him to stand. Thus his position at the table to observe the most number of cards played can be most vital in his play of the game. Also a card caser will want to play at a table that has only a few players, and, better yet, at one where he and dealer meet "head to head." Quite frequently, if house rules permit, a card caser will play more than one hand. In most casinos where this is allowed, a player can bet on an additional hand if there is an unoccupied space, but in some special conditions may be attached. For instance, when the minimum table limit is $1 on a single hand and he wishes to remain at the minimum rate, the second hand would require a $2 bet, or a total bet of $3. But this $3 total minimum on the two hands can be split and, if the player desires, $1.50 may be laid on each. Wagering on a third hand, under similar conditions, calls for a minimum of $5 on the third hand. Again, the wager may be split up any way the player wants just as long as there is at least $1 on each bet and the total comes to $8 or more. In a few casinos the $2 and $5 bets on the second and third hands, respectively, must also be matched by raising the other bets to those amounts. That is, the player has to bet at least $2 on each hand when playing two of them, and at least $5 on each hand when betting on three hands. At the higher minimum tables ($5 and up) there is usually no stipulation on additional hand play, except that you must keep *all* your bets, for each hand played— whether two, three, or more—at the advertised minimum. Remember, the more hands you play, the more control of the card count you have.

The casinos do *everything* to make card casing difficult. When a pit boss suspects a player of casing the deck, he instructs the dealer to reshuffle the deck frequently and not to deal the deck through to the burned card. This, of course, makes counting mor troublesome. If a suspected caser is the only player at the table, the management will generally send in one or two shills to play, or may even "bar" him from the club. With the increasing awareness of the Blackjack player to the value of card casing, several prominent Las Vegas casino executives believe that the use of single deck in their establishment will soon be a thing of the past. The use of multi-decks, dealt in the same manner as a single one, would make casing the cards much more difficult and give them back their house advantage.

Money Management

As with all casino games, money management is important in Blackjack. True, the object of the game is to draw to beat the dealer. But just drawing to beat the dealer will not really let you win. You must bet to beat the house by wagering properly. While wagering the minimum appears to permit you to "string out" a small amount for a period of time, actually it only prolongs the loss of your money. The only way to win at Blackjack, as with all casino games, is to bet to win—when the odds are in your favor.

The most successful method of money management in Black-jack depends on the player's casing the cards and betting heavily in favorable situations. If the deck is "10 and Ace rich" (high plus count), for instance, the odds favor the player and call for a heavy bet. Remember that the "natural" bonus of 50 per cent (3 to 2 odds) is the basic strategy of money management for all smart players. That is, bet more heavily when the probability of obtaining Blackjack is high, and drop out or only bet small amounts at other times. For instance, if the deck has run half way through and no Aces have appeared, then bet heavily. If three Aces have been exposed, however, bet the minimum.

One question many beginners ask the pit bosses is: Can I withdraw a bet already made or change its amount during play? The answer is yes, but under certain *very* specific conditions. If you placed a large bet and then note that the dealer begins to shuffle the cards after your money is down, thus destroying your supposed advantage from card counting, you may withdraw or reduce your bet, if you act quickly. In a single-deck game, once you have been dealt a card, whether you have looked at it or not, your bet as it stands in the hole must remain unchanged except for any permit-ted additional betting by splitting pairs or doubling down, until a decision is reached on the play in progress. In the multiple-deck game, the first card dealt face up to any player freezes all the initial betting action at that table, including bets by players not yet reached by the dealing. Remember that the educated Blackjack player not only knows how to take every possible advantage in the game, but he must believe fully in the winning psychology of good money control detailed fully in Chapter 1.

Blackjack Machines

Early in 1965, a large number of automatic Blackjack machines were installed in many Las Vegas casinos. The machines have a minimum of 25 cents and a maximum of $5. Here are instructions as they appear on the machines:

1. "Automatic Blackjack" is electronically operated using a full simulated fifty-two card dcek—automatically shuffled and dealt. Play is initiated upon the deposit of a coin, or coins, in any or all denominations of quarters, halves or silver dollars . . . to a limitation of five coins of each denomination.

2. The sequence of the game is in accord with all standard "Blackjack" or "21" games.

3. The player has the option of "hitting or standing" on the hand and score dealt. All scores are numerically indicated immediately.

4. The "dealer" will continue to draw cards automatically until it has a score of 17 or more—at this time the score of the player is compared to the "dealer" and payoff is automatically made according to the score and the amount of the bet made. If the player makes a "Blackjack" he receives *double* (2 to 1) his original bet instead of the usual one and a half payoff.

5. "Automatic Blackjack" is fully approved by the Nevada Gaming Commission. All card dealing is absolutely uncontrolled and based upon chance.

6. Any player, after receiving two or more cards showing a score of 10 or 11 may elect to "double down." Simply press the yellow flashing light button, increase your bet in the same denomination up to double your original bet, press the "hit" button, and you will receive one card only to complete your hand.

The electronically operated machines have several *disadvantages* for the "good" Blackjack player. The cards are reshuffled after each hand, the player cannot split pairs, doubling is limited to 10 or 11, casing of the cards is impossible, and the machine play is slow. For these reasons, it is wise to stay away from one of these machines unless you just wish to waste away a few quarters. Remember that your success in Blackjack all depends on your skill in playing and in managing your bets, and your luck.

4

♠

Games of Cards—Poker, Pan, Baccarat

"It's not whether you win or lose, it's how you play the game," may be said for the world of sports, but it has no place in the gambling world, where the most important thing is to win. As for games of cards, the saying should be paraphrased; "Whether you win or lose depends on how you play the game."

In many of Las Vegas' casinos, there are card rooms where you can play Poker and Pan in a comfortable and congenial atmosphere. In these rooms, the casinos either take a fixed percentage—usually 5 per cent—out of the pot or level a tax or charge against each player on each hand. This is reasonable enough, and it pays the casino's overhead and earns the operation a profit. Since both Poker and Pan get fairly good play it is sometimes quite a lot of profit. But, for this fee, the house furnishes the dealer—which is a *most* important point for the "amateur" card-player.

It is a good general rule, especially in Poker, to play *only* in a casino game. At any other location in Las Vegas the average poker-player could be cheated blind by a card sharper. But at a casino, the dealer, who is a professional, keeps the game as honest as possible. You might notice, in a casino game, how closely the dealer will watch the hands of an obvious "smoothy," someone he has spotted as a possible cheater. This fellow usually has super-sharpened fingernails. He will either make a slight scratch on all Aces and big cards as he can in, say, three or four rounds of the cards, or he will use some other identifying mark. The dealer may spot this right off the deal, and when this player tosses a $5 chip out there instead of the $1 one that he has been betting, the dealer will pull the cards and start with a fresh deck. When the pit boss comes by, the dealer will hand him the deck, and nod at the man in question. If the man has been up to some monkey business, he will be barred from the casino for life. Remember that in both Poker and Pan you play against fellow players, *not* the house.

Poker

Poker has become the national card game of the United States because it so well suits the American temperament. It is a game for the individual. In it, the player is on his own, the master of his own fate. There are, of course, other reasons why Poker is such a timeless favorite.

While it is often called the American national game—sharing this distinction with baseball—it is popular throughout the world. While the history of Poker is rather difficult to trace, it combines principles of card games known for centuries in Europe and probably long before that in the Orient, but in its present form it is distinctly of American origin. While no one can prove it, most poker historians believe that our name Poker was derived from the French game of *poque*. This card game was first introduced to our country from France in the early 1800's along the Mississippi River and in New Orleans. It spread throughout the south and southern gentlemen from the cotton plantations—untutored in French pronunciation—decreed that according to its spelling the name should have two syllables. So they changed "poque" to "po-que," or "po-kuh." Later it is believed that the southern pronunciation of the game po-kuh was given a northern touch, and hence Poker.

There is a popular misconception that Poker is just a game of pure luck. Actually, nothing could be further from the truth. Poker is a game of skill, with luck playing only a very minor role in the outcome of any game. Sure you can have a run of bad cards, but the way you play through it is very much the measure of your skill. In other words, if you are losing consistently, you're not unlucky. You're just being outplayed.

Despite the fact that there are innumerable forms of Poker and that the strategy differs slightly in all of them, good players will almost always wind up winners and poor players will almost always wind up losers. But to become a good Poker player, you must learn the art—and it is an art—and skill of Poker. Fortunately, however, the art and skill of Poker is not a matter of years of practice. It has often been stated that to become a first-rate Poker player, you must be one part mathematician, one part economist, and one part psychiatrist. While this is undoubtedly true, as these skills apply to Poker, they can be learned. Not overnight, to be sure, but much more quickly than you might expect. It would be, of course, foolish for a beginner in Poker to sit in on a Las Vegas game. Get your practice in friendly games first.

There are three basic types of Poker—Draw, Stud and Lo-Ball—played in Vegas' casinos. Let's take a look at the strategy of each.

Draw Poker

In this game, five cards are dealt, one at a time in rotation, face down, to each player. There is then a betting interval, after which each active player in turn may discard one or more cards and the dealer serves him that number of cards from the top of the pack, to restore his hand to five cards. (A player need not draw; he may play the cards originally dealt to him, in which case he is said to "stand pat.") After the draw, there is another betting interval, followed by a showdown. The best or highest-ranking hand, of course, wins the pot.

THE POKER HANDS. A poker hand consists of *only* five cards. The value of a hand depends on whether it contains one of the following combinations:

Straight flush, the highest possible hand: all five cards of the same suit and in sequence, as the 5, 6, 7, 8, and 9 of diamonds. The highest-ranking straight flush is the A, K, Q, J and 10 of one suit, called a *royal flush*.

Four of a kind rank next under a straight flush; as four Aces or four 7s. It doesn't matter what the fifth, unmatched card is.

A *full house* is three cards of one rank and two cards of another rank, 9–9–9–3–3, and ranks next under four of a kind.

A *flush* is five cards of the same suit, but not all in sequence, and ranks next below a full house.

A *straight* is five cards in sequence, but not all of the same suit.

It loses to a flush or higher hand, but beats anything else.

Three of a kind rank next under a straight.

Two pair, as K–K–6–6–3, rank next under three of a kind.

One pair beats any hand containing no pair but none of the higher-ranking combinations above.

And below the rank of hands containing one pair are all the no-pair hands, which are rated by the highest card they contain, so that an Ace-high hand will beat a King-high hand, and so on.

Since the most popular form of Draw Poker by far in casinos is that of jackpots (Jacks or better), we will stress the strategy of this game. However, most of the points will apply to every form of Draw Poker.

WHEN TO OPEN. To open the first round of betting in jackpots, as previously stated, a player must have a pair of Jacks or better. The privilege of opening goes to the first player to the left of the dealer and, if he passes, to the next player on the left, and so on until the pot is opened or the deal is passed around and a new one started. But, even if you have openers you have the option of betting or passing. In other words, there are times, depending upon your position (closeness to the dealer) and the number of players in the game, when it may be unwise, even though you have the necessary requirements, to be the first to open.

Most experts agree that in a game with five players or less, you should open the pot even if you just have a pair of Jacks. If you are under the gun (next to the dealer) with six in the game you should pass a pair of Jacks or Queens. In the other positions open with any legal openers. If seven or eight are in the game, the player under the gun shouldn't open on less than Aces; the second and third men should open only on Kings or better; fourth and fifth on Queens; after that on Jacks. Two pairs, however low, are always adequate to open any position. The reason behind the logic of these simple rules is based on the fact that with only four to hear from the chances are that no one will raise you since the probability of better hands is less and there is a chance that a player or two will drop. With more players in the game the chances of winning on a pair of Jacks becomes increasingly poorer and the chances that someone after you will raise your opening bet are very good. If you pass your minimum openers and someone else opens the play, you can stick around to draw to your holding generally with a minimum bet. If someone does not open, there's always another hand, and you must be satisfied to know that you played the hand the way the experts would.

CHANCE OF BEING HIGH IN THE FIRST FIVE CARDS

			Number of Opponents				
Your Hand	1	2	3	4	5	6	7
Three of a Kind	.97	.94	.92	.89	.87	.84	.82
Two Pair	.93	.86	.80	.74	.68	.63	.59
Pair of Aces	.89	.79	.70	.62	.55	.49	.43
Pair of Kings	.88	.78	.69	.61	.54	.48	.42
Pair of Queens	.83	.68	.56	.46	.38	.32	.26
Pair of Jacks	.79	.63	.50	.40	.32	.25	.20

To further validate this strategy, the chart here shows that the chances of being high in the first five cards decreases as the number of players increases: i.e., with three other players in the game the chances of being high with Jacks is 50 per cent, or 2 to 1 odds; with six opponents to worry about the odds raise to 4 to 1 while the percentage decreases to 25. Therefore, in the latter case you need a better hand to win and should not always open on an absolute minimum. There is an old Poker adage that states: High man going into the draw has the best chance of winning the pot. In other words, if, before the opening bet, you are sitting with better cards than your opponents', the odds favor your winning the hand—provided, of course, you stay until the final bet. By using the table just mentioned above and the table below which lists how often you can expect any combination of cards to show up in the first cards dealt, you can get a pretty good idea how your hand rates with opponents' going in.

Ranking order of Hands	*Chances of Being Dealt in the Original Five Cards*	*Number of Possible Ways Hand Can Be Made*
Royal Flush	1 in 649,740	4
Straight Flush	1 in 64,974	36
Four of a Kind	1 in 4,165	624
Full House	1 in 694	3,744
Flush	1 in 509	5,108
Straight	1 in 255	10,200
Three of a Kind	1 in 47	54,912
Two Pairs	1 in 21	123,552
One Pair	1 in 2½	1,098,240
No Pair	1 in 2	1,302,540

Sometimes it is even wise strategy, especially when there are more than five other players, to pass a good hand—three of a kind —under the gun. When someone else opens, you can call and not take over the driver's seat (position of advantage) until after the draw.

POSSIBLE HANDS OF LESS VALUE THAN ONE PAIR

Ace High	502,860
King High	335,580
Queen High	213,180
Jack High	127,500
Ten High	70,380
Nine High	34,680
Eight High	14,280
Seven High	4,080
Total	1,302,540

Staying in. Whether you stay in a hand depends on the cards originally dealt and your chances of improvement through the draw. To help you make your mind on the latter point, the table here should be carefully studied. It reveals the odds against improving any given hand in draw poker, when the rule is "Jacks or better" to open the pot.

As you can see from the chart on page 72, you are best off with a maximum draw: that is, three cards when you have a pair, or two cards when you have three of a kind.

In jackpots it usually is considered very poor Poker strategy to stay in with less than a pair of Jacks and most good players even fold on them, believing that Queens or better are minimum to stay with. To save two unmatched cards and draw a small pair will do absolutely no good. Even if you hold a small pair and catch a second pair—only once in every five draws—you stand a good chance of losing because the odds are all with the players with the better hands. Of course, if you insist on fattening up the pot by playing poor cards, you must expect to lose. The only possible exception to this is when the ante is big due to repeated passes on previous hands. But, even in such cases, do not stay unless the odds the pot is offering are as good or better than the odds of your winning the pot if your draw is successful.

To figure the odds that the pot is offering, or, as it is generally

Cards held in hand	Cards drawn		Odds against making
One pair	3	Two pair	5 to 1
		Three of a kind	8 to 1
		Full house	97 to 1
		Four of a kind	359 to 1
		Any improvement	2½ to 1
One pair with Ace kicker	2	Aces up	7½ to 1
		Another pair	17 to 1
		Three of a kind	12 to 1
		Full House	119 to 1
		Four of a kind	1,080 to 1
		Any improvement	3 to 1
Two pairs	1	Full house	11 to 1
		Any improvement	11 to 1
Three of a kind	2	Full house	15½ to 1
		Four of a kind	22½ to 1
		Any improvement	8½ to 1
Three of a kind and one odd card	2	Full house	14½ to 1
		Four of a kind	46 to 1
		Any improvement	11 to 1
Four-straight, open ends	1	Straight	5 to 1
Four-straight, one end or inside	1	Straight	11 to 1
Four-flush	1	Flush	4½ to 1
Four-straight flush, both ends open	1	Straight flush	22½ to 1
		Any improvement	2 to 1
Four-straight flush, one end or inside	1	Straight flush	46 to 1
		Any improvement	3 to 1
One Ace	4	Pair of Aces	3 to 1
		Aces up	14 to 1

called the *pot odds*, you simply count (roughly) the number of chips in the pot. If, for example, the ante in a six-handed game is one chip, and the two men before you—one opens for two and the other calls for two—have put in four chips, there should be ten chips in the pot when it comes your turn to call. Since you must pay two chips to stay, the pot offers you 5 to 1 odds. Now you should compare the odds against your chances of winning the pot; suppose you have a four-card flush, in which case the odds are 38 to 9, or somewhat more than 4 to 1, that you would not make a flush on a one-card draw. Since the pot offers you 5 to 1, and the odds against your making the flush are only 4 to 1, you should put in the two chips and play. Such calculation is worthless, of course, unless you are virtually sure of winning the pot if your draw is successful. If there is any appreciable danger that you may make the flush and still lose, you should not play. For instance, you should fold in such a pot if it has been raised more than once. The old adage about throwing good money after bad is definitely applicable here. Remember that by checking your chances from the improvement chart (page 72) plus judging your opponents' possible strength, you will be able to determine whether to stay or not.

WHEN TO RAISE. To raise the pot after the betting has been opened is generally done for two reasons: (1) to drive other players out of hand; and (2) to increase the size of the pot. Generally speaking, it is not the best strategy to drive other players out when you think that you have the best hand since poker probabilities show that the best hand going in is a consistent winner. Therefore if you have three of a kind (10s or better) or a pat hand, you should never raise; you should just call, hoping to lure in other players and increase the size of the pot before your good hand is revealed.

In some cases, however, a raise before the draw to drive players out is good strategy. For example, if you have two pair in a seven-hand game, there is a 63 per cent probability (see page 70) that your hand is high before the draw; but the odds are 11 to 1 that you would not improve it. It is standard practice to raise the opener on such a hand, to drive out the other players before they can draw, improve their hands, and perhaps best you. This is especially true in a game in which players make a general habit of staying in with any type of pair, straight, or flush draw. Eliminate as much competition as quickly as possible in such cases.

The exception to this strategy is if you have a high two pairs, such as Aces or Kings up. In this case you do not want to eliminate your competition since you have a good chance of winning even against players who stay and improve, but who get no better than Queens up. As a general rule, however, if you hold a weak two pairs (Jacks up or lower), raise immediately to drive out any players who want to ride along on a cheap hand and also to see if your opponents have better hands than yours. Since a raise has been made, the really good hand—three of a kind and better—will reraise at this point since most of the undecided players will have dropped on the first raise.

When betting or raising it is well to keep in mind that you must conceal your purposes and intentions as best you can. To do this, you must vary betting and raising techniques so as to keep your opponents guessing. It is not necessary to play unsoundly in order to vary your game; there are often several sound methods of playing any particular hand in any given situation. For example, you should sometimes raise before the draw on a good hand; such as three of a kind or better; at other times you should wait, draw one card as though to a straight or flush possibility and then bet after the draw. You should sometimes open the pot on a good hand, and at other times wait until someone else has opened and then raise.

Position play is very important in Poker and occasionally by raising a bet in the opening interval you can create a good position for yourself from one which is naturally bad. For instance, suppose there are two other active players, whom we will call A and B, besides yourself. Player A has opened and Player B has raised. While you have a good hand, very likely the best, you are afraid of both opponents and you can foresee a possible situation after the draw in which A will check to the raiser, B will bet, and you will be caught in a bad position between the two of them. (In casino play, while the dealer remains the same, his position theoretically shifts one player after each deal.)

To rectify your bad position, it may be wise to reraise rather than call since normally A and B will check to you after the draw and, if your hand has not picked up any strength, you can check, too, and get a free showdown. If they check and you have improved your hand, then bet the cards for all they are worth. However, if either of the other two players bets into you after the draw, you can assume that he has improved, and you should drop. Thus making a raise or reraise at this point is most strategic because the betting is usually lower before the draw than after. By making your move here at a low level you save yourself a dangerous call at a higher or more expensive level.

MAKING THE DRAW. When making the draw, you have two purposes: 1) to improve your hand; and 2) to deceive the other players. If your main object is to just improve your hand, your best move is to make the maximum draw: that is, if you have one pair you draw three cards; is you have three of a kind to start with you draw two cards; and if you have two pairs, one card. While sometimes you will need some specific degree of improvement, it may be more important to deceive the other players than to improve your hand. In other words, in the latter case, you hold a kicker to a pair, while with three of a kind you will draw one card and with a high pair up you will stay pat. The advantage of keeping your opponents guessing by varying your play offsets, as just discussed, the lessened chance of improvement. Remember that a winning Poker player is one who occasionally varies his draw.

Many good Poker players, when they have three of a kind, draw just one card, since their chances of winning without improvement are good. When you hold a kicker, you do not represent your hand too strongly before the draw and players with two pairs are likely to at least call you, since a one-card draw usually indicates two pairs, especially when you open.

TWO-CARD DRAW. When you make a two-card draw it advertises to your opponents that you have three of a kind or are holding a pair with an Ace kicker. (Drawing two cards to a plain three-card flush or three-card straight is unsound Poker.) When you hold three of a kind, especially if you have less than four opponents, the odds are all in your favor that you will have the winning hand at the showdown even if you do not improve it. Therefore, while a two-card draw gives you a much better chance to make four of a kind and slightly better chance to show any sort of improvement, in most hands it would not make too much difference if you drew two cards, one card, or even stood pat; you would still win. For this reason, the draw to three of a kind is usually just a matter of personal tactics.

When you keep an Ace kicker with your pair and draw only two instead of three, you reduce your chances of improvement slightly, but such a move does have other compensations—if you want them. For instance, a high pair with an Ace or King kicker is a good combination to hold as a bluff on the chance you do make two pairs and no better. (With a kicker your chances of making two pairs are slightly better than with a three-card draw. Against this, your chances of getting three of a kind dwindles from 1 out of 8 to 1 out of 12.) But you should not use this strategy too often, or you will become tagged and the bluff value will be lost.

THREE-CARD DRAW. A pair is the only logical three-card draw. In some cases, especially when there are only three or four other players, you might draw three cards to an Ace-King of the same suit, and hope for the best. However, all too often you will come out with just what you went in with, a no pair hand with Ace high. If you make a pair of Aces or a pair of Kings, you may beat a player who opened on Jacks or Queens, but never forget that he may have bettered his hand, too. In actual practice, it is usually foolish to draw two unmatched cards, unless the pot odds are very good.

SPLITTING OPENERS. It is permissible to split openers and the face need not be announced. (In some instances, house rules require that a player announce that he is splitting openers and the discard is kept beside him.) For example, let's suppose you open the pot holding DQ, SQ, SJ, S10, S9. With this hand, you wish to take the chance of drawing to the possible straight flush of SQ, SJ, S10, S9. You may then discard the DQ and draw one card. It's generally considered good Poker to split openers to draw to a straight flush, but it's unwise to do it to draw to an ordinary straight or flush. The discards of the opening player should go in the pot, together with the chips, so that the openers may always be demonstrated.

Watching your discards. By studying your discards, you may get some ides how good your hand is or will be. For instance, suppose you were dealt a hand containing Q, Q, A, K, 7. Under most conditions your discard would be the A, K, 7. If you caught another Queen in draw, you could bet your three ladies like they were Aces. Why? Simply because by your discarding the Ace and King the chances of one of the other players having three of them is very remote even if, by chance, he did go in with a pair of Aces or Kings. Thus by remembering your discards, it is often possible to determine to a degree the possibilities of your opponents.

BETTING AFTER THE DRAW. After the draw, you should concern yourself with the answers to these four questions:

1. How did my hand rate against my opponents going in?
2. How many cards did my opponents take in the draw?
3. Did I improve my hand in the draw?
4. Am I playing against conservative or wild players?

The answer to the first question is often answerable by the second. By knowing your opponents' betting patterns before the draw and by knowing the number of cards they took, you should be able to judge approximately the type of hand they are holding and be able to rate yours against theirs. The answer to number three is quite obvious. But, if you have improved your hand to the point where the odds indicate that you will be high man at the showdown, be sure to make your opponents pay through the nose to see what you have got. In such cases, remember the old saying, "Charity begins at home," and play your hand accordingly.

To be successful in betting, you should study and know the habits of the other players in the game. Then, when you think you may have the winning hand, remember how they played their current hands and what type of hands they usually play that way. It is impossible to tell, of course, whether or not they have improved; but you do know that the odds against improvement of any hand runs from 2½ to 1 on up. If you can be fairly certain of the sort of hands they went in with, then you may bet whenever the odds are against their having improved, provided your position is such that you would not run into one or more reraises and be doubtful as to whether you should call or drop. It should not take too long to be able to tag your opponents as either conservative or wild players. As a rule you are safer betting into the conservative player than into the wild player. Also you can make money against the conservative player by betting because you may get a call on a fair hand. On the other hand, you cannot make money against a wild player by betting since he would not generally call if he missed, and he will raise if he hit.

The purpose of the raise before the draw was to drive as many players as possible out of the game. It is unlikely that you will drive out anyone by betting after the draw (anyone, that is, who would not have gone out anyway), and there is no point in your betting unless you have improved your hand to the point where you can beat the probabilities of your opponents. For this reason, it is generally considered dangerous to bet into a one-card draw who can raise and win if he has made a straight or flush, and who probably would not even call if he did not; such a bet stands to lose everything and gain nothing. In other words, a bet at this time is poor Poker because the one-card draws have either busted and will drop, or have filled and will call or raise and probably win. In such a case your best move is to check.

When the opener checks, it generally indicates that he only improved his hand slightly or not at all. If there has been a one-card draw, however, he is probably checking for the reason given above. But, if there has been no one-card draw, and the opener checks, you should bet with two pairs or better unless there are several players at your left who have not been heard from. In this case, it is best to check too unless you have a powerhouse. But, if the opener and several players on your right check, then bet even your two pairs.

If the opener bets after the draw, and you call, and the player on your left raises, drop if the opener calls or reraises, but call if the opener drops. In the latter case, it is your job to keep the bettor honest. But, when calling under other circumstances, remember the old maxim that a good Poker player does not call. Either he has the winning hand and raises, or he has a losing hand and drops. This is an undue oversimplification. Nevertheless, the calling game is usually a losing game. No call should ever be made from curiosity or pique. The only standard for a call is: You should have a better hand than the hand on which the player against you might, in your estimation, have bet. If you find yourself consistently calling and losing, revise your style so that you do not call so often.

Never throw your cards or fold until your turn to bet comes. Premature folding is unfair to the other players in the game.

Stud Poker

There are two major varieties of Stud Poker—five-card stud and seven-card stud—played in Las Vegas' casinos. In Stud Poker, each player receives one or more cards face down—his *hole cards*—and his remaining cards face up. There is a betting interval after each round of face-up cards is dealt, and in seven-card stud, an additional betting interval after the deal of the last cards, which are dealt face down. After the betting is over, the face-down cards are exposed and the best Poker hand wins the pot.

Five-Card Stud Poker Strategy

To be a consistent winner at five-card Stud Poker as well as in other stud games, you must be a keen observer and have a great deal of patience. In this game, your ability to observe and remember what cards have shown and have been folded is the key to your success. If you cannot do this you would not know the chances that a particular opponent has a particular hole card. Also, you would not know your own chance of improving. In other words, when playing Stud Poker—either five- or seven-card—you have to watch everything and remember everything.

The patience involved in Stud Poker playing is of the self-discipline variety. Since most stud games require no ante, you do not have to bet unless you have the high card showing on the first round. Thus you can sit in the game for literally hours and hardly spend any money, just waiting for the good hand to come along. It requires patience to sit in a Poker game and have one poor hand after another, but the winning player must be prepared to do so. It is well to remember that the winnings usually always go to the stud players who are conservative at the start and bold when they think they have the best hands.

Probabilities in Five-Card Stud. In five-card stud you must make your decision to drop, stay or raise, not when you hold five cards, as in draw, but at the moment when the first two cards have been dealt to you. Generally in five-card stud, the average winning hand is the lowest among all forms of Poker—a pair of Kings or a pair of

Aces. Many pots are won on less (such as Ace high) and many pots require more, as the upcards will reveal; but it's a basic principle to stay only when the odds against making two Kings or better are less than the odds offered by the pot. The table here shows your chances, in percentage, of being high at the end of a five-card stud deal with nothing wild. Remember that in most stud games, even with seven or eight players starting, only two or three usually are around to the end.

CHANCES OF BEING HIGH AT THE COMPLETION OF THE DEAL

Your Hand	Number of Opponents						
	1	2	3	4	5	6	7
Three of a Kind	.97	.94	.92	.89	.87	.84	.82
Two Pair	.93	.86	.80	.74	.68	.63	.59
Pair of Aces	.89	.79	.70	.62	.55	.49	.43
Pair of Kings	.88	.78	.69	.61	.54	.48	.42
Pair of Queens	.83	.68	.56	.46	.38	.32	.26
Pair of Jacks	.79	.63	.50	.40	.32	.25	.20
Pair of Tens	.76	.58	.44				
Pair of Nines	.73	.53	.39				
Pair of Eights	.70	.49					
Pair of Sevens	.66	.43					
Pair of Sixes	.63	.40					
Pair of Fives	.60	.36					
Pair of Fours	.57	.32					
Pair of Threes	.53	.28					
Pair of Twos	.50	.25					

Too much has been written about the Stud Poker player's methods of appraising and outguessing his opponents. This is a quality that cannot be taught; one has it or he has not. However, the following six points of strategy will help you in the various phases of the five-card stud game. While these points of strategy do not guarantee that you will win, you are sure to lose if you do not follow them.

1. Stay in the game only when your hand is better than anything showing (will "beat the board"). This is not an infallible rule, of course, but it should be generally followed. Occasionally you may be higher than everyone save the bettor. In such instances it would be best to stay one more round. At the offset of this

section on Stud Poker strategy it was stated that patience was a very important factor in winning. While it may be very boring to sit in a stud game and have to fold one poor hand after another, the chances of winning are poor unless you bet only when you can beat anything showing. In all other cases, you should drop from the game.

2. Under no circumstances should you ever play against a pair showing when you have no pair or a lower pair. This is true regardless of how many cards you may have which, if paired, will best the pair showing. Actually, the number of "over" cards is of no consequence whatsoever. Should he have you beaten at this stage, he will figure that he has you beaten at the end and will take full advantage of this fact in the betting. Also be wary of an open pair showing even though you have it beaten with a higher pair employing your hole card. Always consider that he may possibly have another card of the same rank in the hole. As a rule a good Stud Poker player will attempt to cover up the strength of his hand when all the indications are that some concealed hand is better at this stage than his hand is. In such a case, therefore, your move will depend upon your apraisal of the player and his style, as well as the cards thus far exposed.

3. There is a time-honored Stud Poker adage that says, "Never bet into a possible cinch or 'immortal' hand (a hand which cannot be beaten, regardless of your hole card) when the player with the possible cinch can raise back." Suppose, for example, that your opponent has a pair of eights on the board showing and checks. You have a King showing and a King in the hole (called a pair "back to back," or "wired"). According to the adage you should not bet, since if your opponent's hole card makes three of a kind or two pairs for him, he can raise without fear because you cannot possibly beat him. While it is true that you cannot get into much trouble playing so cautiously as the adage suggests, it is no less true that you will lose a lot of good calls. In other words, this adage should not be too strictly construed because a stud player who never bets into a possible cinch hand will usually lose just as surely as one who always bets when he can beat the board. You must appraise each situation separately, and if on the previous betting and cards exposed you judge that your opponent's showing

cards are the best he can muster, then it is a good idea to bet if you can beat the board. This is especially true when your opponent is showing a four-card flush or straight since the odds are all against his making such a hand.

4. Taking the lead in Stud Poker is accomplished by making the first bet in any given round; or raising another player's bet. If you believe you have the best hand, it is wise to permit another player, if possible, to take the lead. If there is any danger that all the other players will check, then you must bet, it being your only opportunity to build up a good pot. If another player takes the lead and continues to bet each round, it is best to wait until the last round to bump him. By that time you may know for sure if you can definitely win. But if you are high with an open pair, on any round except the last, bet the limit. In the last, check to see where the strength lies. The situation which must be guarded against most carefully is one in which your opponent will be able to best you if his hole card has any value, and you will be too weak even to call if his hole card has no value. In such cases it is foolish to bet your open pair at any time.

5. As previously stated, it is very important for you to watch your opponents' cards most carefully, to know what cards remain in the pack. An Ace, for example, cannot be considered a good hole card if all three of the other Aces, or even two of them, have been exposed.

6. Always conceal your hole card by varying your method of play. For example, you should sometimes raise immediately with a pair back-to-back, and at other times wait until a later round. Also you should sometimes check or call when you have a cinch hand and at other times bet immediately on it. As you gain experience in the game, you will devise further methods of varying your style. Remember that it is just as important in Stud Poker to vary your style as it is in draw. Also guard against any mannerism which may conceal your hole card. Such a little habit as constantly looking at your hole card may suggest to a shrewd player that it is low since you will generally remember a really valuable card and will avoid looking again for fear that another player may catch a glimpse of it. On the other hand, a habit such as stacking chips on top of the hole card may indicate that you have a pair wired.

Seven-Card Stud Poker Strategy

In a sense, seven-card stud can be considered as a cross between five-card stud and Draw Poker. It has the basis of stud but with the element of the draw in that the players get the benefit of extra cards. But, in Draw Poker you receive five cards at the beginning of the game and may draw as many as three more cards after the first betting interval for a total of eight to work out a good hand. However, remember that you cannot reuse your discards, thus you end up the draw still playing only with five cards. In five-card stud you receive five cards and must play them as they are. But in seven-card stud, you have the unique situation of being able to manipulate a total of seven cards all at one time to fill out any five-card combination.

This unique situation of the two extra cards makes seven-card stud a very high-value game amont the Pokers. Figuring percentages in the seven-card game is usually tough for the five-card player. In the seven-card game the average winning hand is a fair three of a kind, such as three eights or above. Furthermore, because the player has seven cards to play around with, straights, flushes, and even full houses are fairly frequent. It is quite possible, after the seventh card has been dealt, for a player to hold a full house without so much as a single pair showing on board, or a straight with up-cards that appear to opposing players as being so far apart that any connection would be seemingly impossible. In other words, seven-card stud is a game of seduction and deception.

Despite the intricate phases of the game, seven-card stud's proper play is comparatively simple and you do not need to resort to close calculations and straight rules of play required in draw and five-card stud. Seven-card stud is generally the most exciting form of the game and thus is most popular in social Poker circles. It is also a game in which you can lose your money rather fast, however, especially if you disregard the basic strategy of play. Let us take a look at some points to remember.

1. The general tactics of betting and raising in seven-card stud are almost identical to those of five-card stud. The only major difference is that it's rather difficult to be sure that you ever have a

cinch hand since with three cards down at the end of the deal the
unexposed combinations are almost limitless. The early bets and
raises follow pretty well the same general pattern in both forms of
Poker. But, at the last card, betting and raising is somewhat a more
risky proposition in seven-card stud. Bluffing and other skulldug-
gery is much less effective on the last card because it is rather
difficult to know when a player may have a legitimate call, regardless of what he has shown or represented in the past rounds.

2. One of the main hazards in seven-card stud is thinking of the
hand ranks as though they were in a five-card or draw game, basing
the estimate on what will win on values that apply only to the
games with fewer cards. You also must guard against overoptimism
and stubbornness to follow the basic Poker percentages. It should
be remembered that very few hands are won in seven-card stud
without improvement as the game progresses. The possible exception to this is if you have a high three of a kind in the first three
cards. In such cases, of course, it is quite possible to win without
improvement. The winning player in this game is one who stays at
the start if he has made a good draw but folds quickly if he has
failed to improve by at least the fifth card. To stay with a pair,
even Aces, against several other players is poor policy. Hands in
seven-card stud usually range so high that one of the other players
almost certainly has a superior hand. But, even in this game, it is
wise to remember the old Draw Poker adage that the best hand
going figures to be the best hand at the showdown. While it does
not happen with the same regularity as in Draw Poker, it pays to
remember the old adage when playing stud.

3. While your chances of improvement are the same, it is
decidedly more advantageous to have both cards of the pair concealed than to have a split pair (one in the hole, the other
face-up). For instance, suppose you have a Queen face-up and
have a pair of 8s in the hole. If you draw another 8 you have three
8s, and no one is likely to suspect it. On the other hand, if you
start with an 8 up and an 8 and Queen in the hole and catch
another 8, you will have a pair showing and the other players are
automatically on guard. If the case card (the last card) of that
rank does not appear, your opponents must keep in mind the
possibility that you have four of a kind, and while this may

occasionally be useful if you wish to attempt a bluff, it is far less important than the fact that it will prevent you from getting any real betting action.

4. As in five-card stud, it is very important in the seven-card variety to watch all of the cards that fall and to remember the cards that are folded during the play. This knowledge, plus the betting patterns of your opponents, is the key to the index of strength of their hands. Remember that often a simple observation can lead you to some very valuable conclusions.

Lo-Ball Poker

The following are the special rules that differentiate Lo-Ball Poker from regular Draw Poker:

Rank of Cards. The Ace is always low. A pair of Aces ranks lower than a pair of deuces.

Rank of Hands. Straights and flushes do *not* count. The lowest hand, therefore, is 5–4–3–2–A, called a *bicycle*, or *wheel.*

POSSIBLE LOW HANDS, WITH ACE LOW

King High	502,860
Queen High	335,580
Jack High	213,180
10 High	127,500
9 High	70,380
8 High	34,680
7 High	14,280
6 High	4,080
Total	1,302,540

First Betting Interval. The dealer and one or two players to his left ante; the sum of their antes equals the limit before the draw. (If the limit is 2, the dealer antes 1 and eldest hand antes 1; if the limit is 5, dealer antes 1, and the two players at his left 2 each.)

The first turn to open goes to the player to the left of the last ante. There is no minimum hand required to open. The betting before the draw is "pass and out"—each player must bet or drop. The antes count toward the amount required to call.

The Draw. A player may draw any nuber of cards, up to five.

The dealer burns a card, face down, before the draw begins. He puts this card under the chips in the pot.

Second Betting Interval. The limit is double the limit before the draw. Checking is permitted, but in some games a player who checks 7-high or better forfeits all interest in chips added to the pot after he checks. (That is, if a player checks 7-high or better, then calls a bet and loses, he loses everything; if he calls a bet and wins, the bettor against him may withdraw his bet.)

POSSIBLE LOW HANDS, ACE LOW, NO STRAIGHTS OR FLUSHES, OUT OF 2,598, 960 POSSIBLE HANDS

		Chance of Holding
10 High	129,528	1 in 20
9 High	71,904	1 in 36
8 High	35,924	1 in 72
7 High	15,384	1 in 169
6 High	5,120	1 in 508
5 High (5–4–3–2–A)	1,024	1 in 2,538
10 High or Lower	258,885	1 in 10

Skillful Play. It is seldom worthwhile to draw to anything worse than a four-card 8-high holding. The average hand after the draw is 10-high. A pat 9-high hand will win more than half the pots, and a 10-high hand will win half the pots, but it is not worthwhile to open on such a hand in an early position unless it also offers a good one-card draw to a 7–4 high or 6-high hand (in case anyone raises).

With a one-card draw to an 8, the odds are 2 to 1 against getting an 8-high hand, even money on having no worse than 10-high. With a one-card draw to a 7, the odds are 3 to 1 against getting a 7-high hand, 2 to 1 against 8-high or better, even money on having no worse than 10-high. A 7-high is even worth a bet after the draw (especially when it cannot legally be checked); a 7–5 high is worth a raise after the draw, provided no one raised before.

The Psychology of Poker

The major problem you face in any Poker game can be put succinctly as follows: Is my hand better than any of my opponents'. This problem of whether or not your hand is superior or inferior to your opponents' isn't so impossible a task as you may first suppose. An expert, indeed, will very seldom be wrong on this point. In fact, some professional players, if they make an error of this nature three or four times in a Poker session, will conclude that their judgment is so poor that evening that they had better abandon the game for the time being.

While Poker psychology—often called Poker intuition—is a rather special aptitude, it is based primarily on a very close analysis of the three basic factors of any player's make-up—habits, character, and temperament. However, the psychology of Poker will vary to such a degree that it is almost impossible to set down any specific binding rules to follow. Actually, your ability of appraising and outguessing your opponents is a special quality that cannot be taught; you either have it or you do not. But, if you have this latent talent you should develop it to the highest possible degree. If the majority of the players in the game are equal or better than you in this ability and can outguess you constantly, you simply should not play in that game.

Every one of us, in spite of our best efforts, generally have certain habits in the way we handle our cards, the manner in which we draw, the speed of making a bet, the way we stack chips on the hole cards, etc. While you should make every effort to eliminate your telltale traits, you should make every effort to use to your benefit these actions when made by your opponents. They very often might give a good clue to the strength of their hands. A long hesitation before a bet, for example, suggests a bluff, or a slow call suggests a degree of doubt. Betting high quickly or with marked deliberation, on the other hand, can be taken generally to mean a real strong hand.

As a rule, most Poker players have a definite pattern of play, or character as it is often called. By this we mean that all of us have more or less a system of standards to bet, draw, drop, raise, and even bluff. As was stated earlier, it is wise to vary one's game from time to time to prevent other players from being able to read your own game. But you should study the standards of your opponents whenever possible. The best time to do this is when you have folded early and can watch the pattern of play of your opponents who are still in the game. Look at all hands after the call and not just the winner. When a man who raised early is beaten at the showdown, see what he raised on—provided of course the hand was bet and called or checked out so that you have the right to see his holding, regardless of whether it won. It will help you form a mental picture of his character of play. In other words, character is manifested by a player's system of card values and bets.

Most Poker players fall into certain categories that are usually fairly easy to spot. The easiest way to classify your opponents is to ask yourself the following about each player in the game:

1. Does he have any give-away habits?
2. What are his betting, raising and calling standards?
3. Is he a loose or a conservative player?
4. Has he a "poker-face" or does he show his emotions easily?
5. Does he vary his game?
6. Is he a player that is noted to bluff frequently?

Properly correlated the answers will help you to develop your skill in the psychology of Poker. Remember, Las Vegas is no place to "learn" Poker. If you are not an "expert," with a *thorough* knowledge of all odds, it is wise to avoid the game. Even if you are the Friday-night Poker champ in your hometown, remember that casino Poker is the "big leagues." At just about every Poker table there is usually one person who earns his livelihood by winning from the tourist. To him, Poker is not a game of luck, but one of skill. Unless you plan to play by the odds and use Poker psychology to the utmost, do *not* take part in the game at Vegas.

Pan

Pan has suddenly become one of the most popular card games in the "Fun Capital of the World." This game, whose rightful name is *Panguingue*, is derived from *Conquian*, the father of all Rummy card games.

The fascination and excitement in playing Pan comes from the fact that it is played with eight decks of cards, from which the 8s, 9s and 10s have been removed. (Most casinos in Las Vegas also remove one full suit of spades, making a total of 310 cards in the game.) Thus, the 7 is in sequence with the Jack, and the Ace ranks low, below the deuce. Because of the number of cards in the game, they are kept in a wooden box called a "shoe."

In most casinos, an ante of one chip is required before the game starts. (Chips are valued generally at 25 cents, 50 cents, and $1—that is, there are quarter games, half-dollar games, and one-dollar games.) After the cards have been shuffled together, the permanent dealer (he is furnished by the house) takes a sufficient number from the top of the stock to deal each player ten cards, five at a time. (Preserving the tradition of Conquian, the rotation of deal and play is to the *right*, instead of to the left as in most other games.) Any cards left over after the deal are returned to the stock or dealing shoe, and the top card is then turned face up on the table beside the stock for the first player (eldest hand) to decide whether he will use it or draw the top card from the stock or shoe. The winner of the previous hand is considered the eldest hand and thus receives the first card of the deal and makes the first play. In theory, the player to the left of the previous winner is the dealer. The actual dealing, of course, is done by the house.

When the cards are dealt, each player sorts his hand into sequences and triplets (three of a kind), and determines what cards he wants to complete his runs, so that he may be on the lookout for them. The player then draws the top card from the stock and turns it face up on the pack. If this card can be used in combination with any of those in his hand, he draws it over to his side of the table, and takes from his hand the cards completing the combination of three cards, leaving them all face up. Even if he has cards enough in his hand to increase the combination to four or more cards, he should not show them. The cards drawn from the stock must *never* be taken into the hand.

Let us suppose the pone holds these cards: H J 7 6 4; C 5 3 2; D K 7 5; and that the H 5 is the first card he draws. He can use this card in three ways: By making a run of three with the H 4 and H 6; or a run with the H 6 and H 7; or a triplet with the two other 5s. In this case he would probably lay out the 6 and 7, and make the run of three. If he should draw the H Q later on, he could use it by continuing the sequence with his Jack; or if the H 3 appeared, he could use it with his H 4.

If he cannot use the card drawn, or does not wish to, he draws it from its position on the top of the stock and places it between himself and the player to his immediate right still face up. This player then decides whether or not he wants it, and if he does not he "passes" it by turning it face down, and pushing it to his right. Cards once passed in this manner cannot again be seen by either player. The player who passes the card turns up the next one on the stock. If he does not want it, he places it on the table between himself and his adversary, and if his adversary does not want it either, he turns it down and passes it to the pile of deadwood (discards), turning up the top card of the stock again. In this manner it will be seen that each player has to decide on two cards in succession; the one drawn but not used by his adversary, and the one he draws himself. This is continued until a player "goes out."

If a player uses any card drawn from the stock in this manner, it is obvious that he has too many cards, and in order to reduce his hand and show-downs to ten cards, he must discard something, unless he can show down everything remaining in his hand, in which case he would have eleven cards down, and win the game. In discarding, the card thrown out is placed at the disposal of the adversary, as if it were the card drawn from the stock, and if the adversary does not want it, he passes it and draws another. It should be observed that the player drawing the card from the stock always has the first refusal of it. This is sometimes very important, as both players often need the same card.

In the foregoing example, the player's best discard would be his D K, which is too far removed from the others in the suit to make a run possible, and there is no mate to it with which to start a triplet. If the adversary could use this King, he would have to discard in his turn, and the card so thrown out would be at the disposal of the other player, just as if it had been drawn from the stock.

A meld, as in all Rummy games, may be either a group of three cards of the same rank (such as three 4s) or a sequence of three cards in the same suit (such as D 4, 5, 6). Only three cards may be melded in the original set. But a player may add to his own melds (not to melds of other players).

The regulations in full are as follows:

Any three Aces or any three Kings, regardless of suits, form a valid set. These ranks are called *non-comoquers*. Any card of the same rank may be added to a non-comoquer set, regardless of its suit. All other ranks are *comoquers*, and a set here must be three cards of different suits or all of the same suit. To a set of cards in different suits may be added other cards of the same rank in any suit. To a set of cards all in the same suit may be added only cards that are the same in suit as well as rank. A sequence may be added to until the limit of the rank is reached, King high or Ace low.

Conditions, or pays, are certain melds for which the player immediately collects from every other active player. In the description below, *valle* (pay) *cards* refers to 3s, 5s, and 7s. The conditions are:

Three 3s, 5s, or 7s of different suits . . . . .pays 1 chip.
Three 3s, 5s, or 7s of the same suit . . . . .pays 2 chips.
Spades . . . . .pays 4 chips.
Any other three cards in the same denomination in
     the same suit . . . . .pays 1 chip.
Spades . . . . .pays 2 chips.
Jack, Queen, King or Ace, Deuce, Trey of the same
     suit . . . . .pays 1 chip.
Spades . . . . .pays 2 chips.

In the course of adding cards to his melds, a player may split one meld into two, provided that each remains a valid meld, and may borrow from an amplified meld to make a new one, under the same proviso. Conditions, or pays, made by splitting or borrowing collect as though they were entirely new. Each card added to a condition collects anew for the entire condition.

The first player to meld exactly eleven cards wins the deal. Since the original hand of ten cards cannot be increased, this means that the winner at his last turn draws a card, melds it, and does not discard. A player may meld all his ten cards and have none left; in this case he continues to draw and discard until he draws a card that he can lay off. An important (an exasperating) rule is that if a discard fits with a meld of the in-turn player, he must draw it and meld it on demand of any other player. The object in making this demand is to make it more difficult for the victim to go out. If he holds two cards, which may be a pair, his chances of going out are reduced if he has to break up his pair. For instance, a player has eight cards down, two sequences of four small cards each, and in his hand a pair of Kings will make him game; but if he has to depend on his sequences to put him out, he will have to get three more cards. (Remember that the player must "go out" with 11 cards.) Suppose he draws a card that will fit one of his sequences; it is to his advantage to pass it; but upon laying it on the table any of the active players in the game at that time (players who have dropped out at beginning of the game are not considered active) may force him to take the card by placing it at the end of his sequence, at the same time saying: "Discard." The player must follow his adversary's order.

In the same manner, if the card drawn fits into a showdown sequence of his adversary to his immediate right, he or any of the active members in the game can force that player to take the card and discard one from his hand. Also a player holding one of the cards of his immediate right adversary's show-down sequence or triplet may force after using a card, by placing his discard on this adversary's sequence, instead of laying it on the table. If it is laid on the table, the adversary may, if not forced at once by an active player, turn it down, and it is then too late to compel him to use it. Suppose, for example, you think your adversary to the right holds two cards of an unplayed sequence, and has a triplet on the table. If you can use one of those sequence cards in his hand to advantage, and can force him by giving him the fourth card of his triplet, which is of no use to you, by all means do so; but you must remember that you cannot force in such a case except after using a card yourself, because you are not allowed to discard under any other circumstances.

The player who first "goes out" collects two chips from all of the active players, as well as collecting again for all the pay "spreads" in his hand. The ante is also taken by the winner. As a general rule, conditions or pay spreads are collected when the meld is made. The dealer, as in Poker, takes the house's cut of the pot, which is usually 5 per cent of the total earnings.

A player who has an incorrect hand may have it replaced with a new hand before he makes his first play; thereafter an incorrect, or foul, hand is dead but the holder must make all payments as though he were still in the game. If he has made any collections for conditions, he must return them.

An illegal meld must be made legal when attention is called to it; if the player cannot make it legal, the penalty is the same as for an incorrect hand. No play is final until a player has discarded. If a player picks up a drawn card and puts it in his hand, this move also constitutes an incorrect, or foul, hand. The dealer's decision is always final in all cases of house rules.

Pan as played at most casinos is not a "blood" game like Poker. As Rudy Lauber, who runs the Pan games at the Sahara, told us: "Pan is a game where—with average luck and knowledge—you can play for a whole night without 'getting hurt too bad.' In a quarter game, for instance, I would say $20 won or lost would be considerable money. This is true for the big games, too—$40 in a 50-cent game, $80 in a $1 one. You can have a lot of fun at Pan without costing you a lot of money."

Baccaràt/Chemin de Fer

A game with a history that goes back to the Court of Charles VII in the late 15th century, Baccarat/Chemin de Fer was introduced to America in the early 1900's but its popularity was short-lived when, a year or two later, Blackjack made its debut. It was re-introduced in Vegas in 1958 and it has been increasing in popularity ever since. The game has an *average* house advantage of 1.15 per cent and is about the simplest game to play in town.

Up to twelve players can play Baccarat at one time and they sit at an oval table slotted in the center to accommodate the croupier, or dealer. The numbers that appear on the table layout represent the seat numbers of the players. Baccarat is generally played for cash—with a minimum of $5 to $20, and a maximum of $2,000. The house banks the entire game and a money-dealer collects losing wagers and pays off winners. He also keeps track of the 5 per cent commission levied on bank bets.

In Baccarat, only two hands are dealt—a player's hand and banker's hand. Strict rules determine its play so that the player does not have to make any decisions other than the size of his wager and whether to bet on the player's hand or the bank's. Bets with the player's hand are made by placing the money in front of your position in the area marked "Player." Wagers with the bank are placed in the "Banker" area in the section marked with your position number. There is no strategy that can be used to increase your chances of winning and, because it is a game of pure chance, the house advantage against bets with the player is only 1.23 per cent, and only 1.06 per cent for bets with the banker.

Baccarat is played with eight decks of cards. The cards are shuffled by the players—reshuffled by the croupier. He then inserts a blank white card six cards from the bottom of the pack. The pack is then placed in a wooden dealing shoe. The purpose of the white card is to show the croupier that only one more hand can be dealt before the cards must be reshuffled.

At the start, the bank is designated at position 1, and the player at this location deals from the shoe one card at a time face down until he has given two cards to the croupier and two cards to himself. The croupier will then hand the cards, as a matter of courtesy, to the player to the banker's right who is betting the highest amount of money against the bank (for the player). These two cards are turned over and exposed to all; at the same time the croupier calls out the player's count. Then the banker looks at his cards and turns them over for the croupier to call out the bank's total. These card totals dictate the action that follows; the player or banker has no decisions to make. The following are rules that are used in Las Vegas casinos:

RULES FOR THE PLAYER

Total of Cards Held *	Action To Be Taken
0–1–2–3–4–5	The Player is given an additional card.
6–7	Player must stand.
8–9	A natural—Player stands—Bank cannot draw.

RULES FOR THE BANKER

Total of Cards Held*	Draws When Giving	Stands When Giving
0–1–2	1–2–3–4–5–6–7–9–10	8
4	2–3–4–5–6–7	1–8–9–10
5	4–5–6–7	1–2–3–8–9–10
6	6–7	1–2–3–4–5–8–9–10
7	Always stands regardless of player's action.	
8–9	A natural—Banker stands—Player cannot draw.	

Note: If a player stands, the banker will draw if his hand totals 5 or lower; he will stand on 6 or higher

* Picture cards and 10s count as zero. For a total in excess of 10, the ten digit is ignored so that the count is always between 0 and 9. For example, $7 + 8 = 15 - 10 = 5$ total card count.

The object of the game is to come closest to the number 9. As we noted, picture cards and tens, and any combination of cards totaling 10, count nothing. Ace is counted one, deuce is counted two, etc. In case of a "tie," the hand is played over.

There is no need for you to memorize the rules, the croupier controls the game completely and tells the banker when to give the player or himself another card. The banker does not deal any cards except at the croupier's direction. All wagers with either the bank or with the player are, as previously stated, made against the house on an even money (1 to 1) basis. The house takes 5 per cent of winning bets made against the player. No percentage is taken of losing banker bet or bets with the player. The house advantage of 1.06 to 1.23 per cent includes the effect of this house commission; otherwise the banker would have an even greater advantage over the player. But despite the fact that that the best bet in Baccarat is to play with the bank, professional gamblers usually play both sides with equal frequency since the difference is only 1.17 per cent.

If the banker makes a "pass" and wins, he retains the shoe and deals again. When the banker loses, the shoe moves to the player on the right, thus giving each player a chance to handle the shoe, or deal. A player may pass the shoe at any time. Incidentally when you are the banker, you can bet either way—with the bank or with the player. You do not have to bet the bank. After the play of a game, the cards of both hands are placed in the discard chute.

While no private wagering is permitted, a few casinos offer side bets to the player. One of these is marked "Nine and Ten" and a bet on it means that the player is betting that the banker will make a nine on his first two cards and the payoff is at 10 for 1, or 9 to 1. Since the correct odds are approximately 9½ to 1 against this being the case, the house advantage is 5.1 per cent. A similar bet pays 9 to 1, or 10 for 1, if the total is 8, and the house percentage is approximately the same as for the bet on 9. Finally, a 4 to 1, or 5 for 1, payoff is offered if the banker's two-card total is either 8 or 9. Again, essentially the same house advantage applies. Thus, it is obvious that these side bets are best left alone.

Baccarat is a fairly fast game—about two hands a minute—and it is one of the best games for beginners; it is just as simple as slot machine play and the odds for winning are a *great* deal better. Actually, the only people who are not overly fond of Baccarat are the casino operators. Some of old-time owners are very leery of the game because the small house advantage makes it extremely difficult for the casino to recoup really big losses that can occur in this game.